A MIRROR OF THE
MINISTRY IN MODERN NOVELS

A MIRROR OF THE

MINISTRY

IN MODERN NOVELS

HORTON DAVIES

Essay Index Reprint Series

 BOOKS FOR LIBRARIES PRESS
FREEPORT, NEW YORK

The publisher gratefully acknowledges' permission to reprint quotations from the work of the following authors:

Balthasar, Hans Urs von: *Le Chrétien Bernanos,* quoted by permission of Jakob Hegner Verlag, Cologne.

Bernanos, Georges: *The Diary of a Country Priest,* translated by Pamela Morris, copyright 1937 by The Macmillan Company; quoted by permission of The Macmillan Company and Librairie Plon, Paris.

Cormeau, Nelly: *L'Art de François Mauriac,* quoted by permission of Éditions Bernard Grasset, Paris.

Cozzens, James Gould: *Men and Brethren,* copyright 1936 by James Gould Cozzens; *By Love Possessed,* copyright 1957 by James Gould Cozzens; both quoted by permission of Harcourt, Brace and Company, Inc.

Cronin, A. J.: *The Keys of the Kingdom,* copyright 1941 by A. J. Cronin; *Grand Canary, copyright* 1933 by A. J. Cronin; both quoted by permission of Little, Brown and Company, Mr. A. J. Cronin, and Victor Gollancz, Ltd.

De Vries, Peter: *The Mackerel Plaza,* copyright 1958 by Peter De Vries; quoted by permission of Little, Brown and Company.

Greene, Graham: *Brighton Rock,* copyright 1938 by Graham Greene; *The Lawless Roads* (published in U.S.A. as *Another Mexico*), copyright 1939 by Graham Greene; *The Power and The Glory,* copyright 1940 by Graham Greene; all quoted by permission of The Viking Press, Inc. and Laurence Pollinger Ltd., London.

STANDARD BOOK NUMBER:

8369-1601-8

LIBRARY OF CONGRESS CATALOG CARD NUMBER:

70-111824

PRINTED IN THE UNITED STATES OF AMERICA

TABLE OF CONTENTS

Prefatory Note and Acknowledgments

Some explanation is surely required for a teacher of religion in a university presuming to indulge in literary criticism. It will be found in my previous education and in my present avocation. English literature was my first love and the embryo of the present book could be found in the essay, 'The Clerical Character in English Literature,' which the writer was required to prepare while an undergraduate reading for the Honours degree in English Language and Literature at the University of Edinburgh, at the suggestion of Professor (afterwards Sir) Herbert Grierson, that great interpreter of the poems of John Donne and the novels of Sir Walter Scott, to whom I shall always be grateful for repudiating the shallow doctrine of 'literature for literature's sake.'

My present avocation as a teacher of the history of Christianity in the Department of Religion in Princeton University brings me in touch with lively undergraduate and graduate students who are reading theology, not in preparation for the ministry, but as a clue to the understanding of the inspirational and fructifying role that religion has played and still plays in the development of our Western civilization.

They are encouraged to correlate their religious understanding with history, politics, art, architecture, philosophy, and—not least—literature. In this free and undogmatic atmosphere I have been encouraged to develop my interest and to share theirs in the correlation of Christianity and culture. It has been particularly interesting for an Englishman to see the vigor and variety of American religion not only with his own eyes, but with the eyes of the American novelists, whether they be visionary or merely jaundiced. In this survey of the portraits of the priest or minister from 1850 to the present day, it is hoped that Americans and Englishmen, the ministry and the laity, will identify themselves imaginatively with this gallery of clerical characters and the Christian communities which they serve so variously, provided by fifteen novelists, seven of whom are Americans, five English, two French, and one a South African. Since these parsons are representatives of the Roman Catholic, Anglican and Protestant Episcopal, Congregational, Methodist, Baptist, Unitarian, and Seventh Day Adventist communions, the experience may be of some ecumenical value.

It is a pleasure to be able to record my gratitude to my colleagues in the Department of Religion at Princeton University, whose generous friendship to the immigrant makes them like so many statuettes of Liberty in their welcomes, and I particularly value the interest of Dr. George F. Thomas, Professor of Religion, virtual founder as well as first Chairman of the Department (1946–59), for I have benefited greatly from his combination of religious, philosophical, and literary insights. I also wish to thank Professor Leland Jamison, Chairman of the Department of Religion at Syracuse University, on whose enthusiastic, even ebullient, knowledge of American religion and novels I have drawn for some suggestions. I am also grateful to have had the benefit of the advice of Professor Edward D. Sullivan, Chairman of the Department of Romance Languages, and Professor Louis A. Landa of the Department of English, both of Princeton University. I am happy to have this opportunity of expressing my gratitude also to Mrs. Joel Nystrom, the friendly and efficient secretary of the Department of Religion, for assistance with the typing, which was rendered with her customary courteous alacrity. Some of my graduate students took a proper concern in educating their educator and provided me with three titles among the twenty novels selected. My wife, as always, cheers me with a charity that throws judgment to the winds, and so sets a fine example to my critics.

H. D.

Princeton, New Jersey
June 1959

I

Reflections and Distortions

THE profession of the priest or minister is full of paradoxes. The minister stands in the public pulpit inculcating the essentially private virtue of humility. Learned in sacred theology, he yet admits that the simple Christian's love in its importance exceeds all his lore. Trained to interpret the needs of modern man with the assistance of psychology and sociology, he stands at the apex of civilization in the Western world, and yet claims that the profoundest revelation of God's truth is to be found in first-century Palestine in Jesus of Nazareth. Believing that Christianity is essentially a practical way of life, of transformed human relationships, of words-made-flesh in dependence on *the* Word-made-flesh, he is professionally a public speaker, an expert in verbalism. He inculcates a perfectionist ethic unattainable in this world, yet proclaims its relevance. The servant of a homeless carpenter who rode upon a borrowed ass, he receives, in addition to his stipend, a parsonage or a presbytery free of rent, and a travel allowance for an automobile. Accused of hypocrisy, sentimentalism, obscurantism, and irrelevance by the era of Relativity, he is yet his own severest critic, when unblinded by the adulation of his admirers.

3

THE CHIEF PARADOX

He knows that his task is impossible. This is the paradox of paradoxes: that he as finite, fallible, and sinful man has to represent the infinite and Holy God. His problem is more difficult than that of ancient priests, prophets, and sages, if he is a Christian priest or minister, and yet it is also easier. Easy, in that he is not required to guess at the nature of God from the inferences he can draw from the nature of the universe, for in the resulting ambiguities of such guesswork he might escape from God, as it were in the mists of uncertainty; yet the task is also difficult because the very concreteness of the Divine revelation to which he witnesses—the Incarnate God—is so demanding in His claims. The ultimate paradox is indeed this— that God has entrusted the treasure of His Gospel to the earthen vessel of the minister's personality. He is to reflect the restored and perfected image of God in Christ, the New Adam, the *icon* of the invisible God. Yet his pride, his fear, his fallibility, his rebellion, are always distorting the reflection of that image. The function of the clerical characters drawn by the novelist is to rebuke the minister for the distortions of the image of Christ and to encourage him by the more faithful reflections of the same image.

In the long course of the Christian centuries, the priest or minister has fulfilled his dual office of representing God to the people and representing the people before God in different ways and with varying emphases. In the early centuries, especially after the sack of Rome and the consequent disintegration of that great empire in the fifth century, he was chiefly a director of souls. Today, by contrast, he seems to be—especially in the city centers—a spiritual executive, the director of a religious community that works by committees and often with a team of specialists in education, music, and psychiatry. In all ages, however, he has had certain basic functions to perform, however differently their importance has been assessed from century to century. Almost always he has had to preach the Gospel of the grace of God as both mercy and judgment, promise and condemnation; to instruct the young in Christian doctrine and behavior; to lead that grateful homage of the people to God which is worship; and to administer those sacraments which mark significant stages in the development of the human life in relation to God; to be the spiritual counsellor of all anxious souls; and often he has been required to act as God's distributor of charity in a needy world. His task is not fundamentally different in the present day, though the foes of the faith may take a new and menacing form and the varieties of the ministry in education, social welfare, institutional chaplaincies in schools, prisons, hospitals, and the armed forces, may require specialized knowledge and experience.

The estimates of a minister's or priest's work have varied historically with the outlook of the age and with the viewpoint of the observer. English and American literature have preserved a fascinating series of portraits of the ministry in poetry, drama, and novels. Some are profoundly sympathetic, such as Chaucer's 'poor parson' in *The Canterbury Tales* or Goldsmith's in *The Deserted Village;* others, like Chaucer's Nun's Priest, Milton's 'blind mouths' in *Lycidas,* Cowper's vain coxcombs in *The Task,* and the worldlings of Anthony Trollope's Barchester series of novels, are harshly critical studies of failures in a holy vocation.

THE NOVELIST AND HIS MOTIVES

Our concern will be with estimates of the ministry and the priesthood in the last hundred years. It is significant that the ministry still has its admirers and critics in the novelists of the twentieth century, even though the minister's role has greatly diminished in terms of public recognition. The development of the modern welfare state has taken from the hands of ecclesiastics many duties that would now be considered entirely secular in nature, such as fell to his lot as an educator, a social welfare worker, and a distributor of alms. A new and exacting profession, that of the psychiatrist, has taken over much of his central responsibility as a counsellor to perplexed people. Yet, in a world of relativities, he still retains his relevance in pointing to that intersection of Eternity and time where God became Man and hallowed our human strivings; and in a world of agonizing antagonisms between classes and races his traditional reconciling role is not less but more necessary today; and even in a social welfare world where individuals become ciphers, mere 'cases,' men and women value all the more the concern of this family friend; moreover, in a world of vast aggregations of moving populations, of the decline of craftsmanship and the decreasing significance of creative work in the anonymity of an assembly line, and as rootless inhabitants of sanitary slums or of monotonous mass-produced suburban split-levels, they need a community of ultimate concern such as the Church of Christ is. Above all they need the direction and purpose that come from a life lived under the rule and power of God, whether they realize it or not. It is for these ends a minister exists today.

While modern novels give pride of place to the doctors, the scientists, the engineers, and even the civil servants of today,* they have not entirely neglected the ministry or the priesthood. Indeed, the so-called 'Catholic Renaissance' has provided a renewed and deep understanding of the role of the Catholic priest in the modern world, particularly in England and America, in France and Italy. This can be amply corroborated from

* The reference is to the distinguished novels of C. P. Snow.

the novels and short stories of G. K. Chesterton, Graham Greene, Evelyn Waugh, and A. J. Cronin in England, as from the work of Willa Cather, Thornton Wilder, and Henry Morton Robinson in the United States. The most popular writer on the subject of the priesthood in Italy is the whimsical author of the Don Camillo series of books, Guareschi. In France there are unsurpassed interpretations of the Catholic priest in the novels of Georges Bernanos and of François Mauriac.

The Protestant minister and especially the Protestant missionary have not been treated with similar understanding. In fact, in the English-speaking world the most understanding portraits of the minister's role have come from South Africa and the United States in the work, respectively, of Alan Paton, James Street, and James Gould Cozzens.* The most vituperative criticisms of the Protestant servant of God in the English language have come from the pens of Somerset Maugham and Sinclair Lewis, and the most scintillating satire on the ministry since Swift and Samuel Butler derives from Peter De Vries.

Both appreciation and ridicule have their important functions in enabling the reader to understand better the role of the minister in the modern world. Fiction is able to hold the mirror out to the minister or priest, and to those who avail themselves of their services, these mirrors supply an objective critique otherwise denied to those who are safely ensconced within the admiring fold. Sometimes the satirist himself is appealing to his vision of the Christ behind the Christianity distorted in a clergyman's character, even if, as in Upton Sinclair's case in *The Carpenter*, he overstresses one aspect of the life work of Jesus of

---

* The lack of a sympathetic account of a Protestant minister in the contemporary English novel has been made good in the posthumously published, *The Captive and the Free* (Harper, New York, 1959) by Joyce Cary, which contrasts Preedy, an evangelist and faith-healer, with Syson, an Anglican curate, and ex-fighter pilot, who is as intelligent as he is compassionate, and credible, too.

Nazareth. Sometimes the novelist's very vindictiveness is an anguished cry because he has lost the faith that once gave a pattern to the maze of life, as seems to be the case of Thomas Hardy in *Tess of the D'Urbervilles* and of Somerset Maugham in *Of Human Bondage*. Sometimes, indeed, the critic is the prophet announcing the doom of a compromising and conforming Christianity which has only a gospel accommodated to the vagaries of contemporary culture and is a thinly disguised and dishonest humanism, as one might interpret Peter De Vries' *The Mackerel Plaza.*

Since complacency is the chief enemy of the Christian Church, the critical novelist, whether this is his intention or not, can play the Socratic role of a gadfly, stinging the comatose Church into awareness of its dangerous condition. The benefits of such criticisms come chiefly to the priests and ministers themselves, who are so often surrounded by coteries whose sentimental adulation blinds the recipients to the possibility of greater fidelity to their vocation, or who have become hidebound by the pressures toward conservatism and convention exerted on them by the unimaginative bulk of their congregations.

Moreover, it is as well that priests and ministers, and churchmen generally, should be aware of what their critics are saying, even if they should entirely mistake the proper function of Church and ministry. Churchmen worth their salt will no more than Milton 'praise a fugitive and cloistered virtue.' For ministers themselves, no writer can help them more than the man who often reminds them of the dangers of spiritual pride; and quite unintentionally a severely critical novelist or playwright may help to perform the work of the God who pulls down the mighty from their seats and exalts the humble and the meek.

To be quite specific, one might ask whether a pompous and crassly insensitive minister could remain unmoved after sitting through a performance of Tennessee Williams' *Cat on a Hot Tin Roof*, unless he were wholly anaesthetized by conceit? The Rev. Mr. Tooker is the very embodiment of an opinionated and tactless parasite, a ghastly irrelevance and irreverence while visiting a doomed family in the capacity of friend. If a minister could not recognize himself in the exaggerated portrait, he might at least see that his plain duty in such a situation would be to break down the conspiracy of ineffectual lying that clutches at the throats of the family like a fog, and to proclaim to them the compassion, the forgiveness, and the eternal hope of a Gospel of the Cross and Resurrection.

On the other hand, the novelist who wishes to write a sympathetic account of the sacred ministry and of the Church also performs a valuable service. He may be able to encourage the minister to continue, for example, in the uncalculating path of a reckless compassion for society's derelicts, instead of capitulating to the customary 'hands-off' attitude of conventional church opinion. That, at least, seems a fair inference from James Gould Cozzens' admiration for Ernest Cudlipp of *Men and Brethren* in his fight against the respectable expediency urged by his Rector, Dr. Lamb. In the same way, James Street's small-town sagas of the life of an honest and compassionate Baptist minister, London Wingo (as in *The Gauntlet* and *The High Calling*), are in part an attempt to encourage a minister to persist in speaking out his convictions despite the petty but powerful counterpressures of his congregation. It is also Street's intention to plead for a deeper understanding of the numerous, but often unappreciated, Southern Baptists of America, as the 'Plain People' with their own ethos and important role to play in American life at the grass-roots level.

In François Mauriac and in Graham Greene there are important apologetical motives present. M. Mauriac in the character of Abbé Calou in *La Pharisienne* (also Bernanos in his

Diary of a Country Priest) wishes to show that the man who is regarded as an ecclesiastical failure as a priest, is, in God's eyes, a supreme success, for he is utterly empty of any ambition save that of serving Christ. By this method Mauriac and Bernanos convict the conventional priesthood of a betrayal of their Master, and the community that appreciates such a conventional type of priesthood they arraign as arrant Laodiceans. Graham Greene shows in *The Power and the Glory*, albeit in a most dramatic and often exaggerated form, the remarkable and subterranean providence of God even in atheistic Mexico; stresses the objectivity of the sacraments in a way that would have delighted the anti-Donatistical St. Augustine of Hippo; and prepares his fellow-Catholics living in an apparently God-forsaken world to gird their loins for the second Dark or Darker Ages.

Whether the intention of the novelist be criticism or appreciation, or a combination of the two, the portrayals of the priesthood and the ministry considered in the following chapters are evidence of the continued impact of the holy ministry on the modern world, and they have an intrinsic interest for believer and unbeliever alike.

THE TYPES OF MINISTRY

The selections have been made with a view to showing the image the minister reflects or distorts in the modern world in contemporary fiction. The classification, with its five sections, is not intended to be a watertight division, implying that there are five types of sacred service and no others, or even that one man belongs exclusively to one type. On the other hand, some men have been chiefly preachers or evangelists, some interpreters, some directors of souls, some missionaries, and some community leaders.

1. Preachers and Evangelists

The first three novelists, Hawthorne, Sinclair Lewis, and James Street, have been selected to illustrate the importance they give to the primary role of preaching in the Protestant ministry. Hawthorne's classic *The Scarlet Letter* reflects the first colonial century in American history when the Protestant leader was given the full status of his title as 'Minister of the Word of God.' No people have esteemed the ordinance of preaching as highly as the Puritans. Highly critical of the contemporary seventeenth-century preaching of the Anglican Church from which they dissented, as offering either mere standardized homilies or as prone to ostentation in the form of farfetched etymological textual analysis in Greek, Hebrew, and Latin (as in Bishop Lancelot Andrewes) or in the form of farfetched metaphors or metaphysical conceits in the preaching of Dean John Donne of St. Paul's Cathedral. They considered they were over-reaching themselves if they were not constantly under the orders of the Divine Word of the Scriptures. The most admired Puritan epithet for preaching was 'painful'—that is, preaching that took great pains to apply the Revelation of God to the condition of the people with smarting relevance. Richard Baxter, Puritan preacher par excellence, described the urgency of his task thus:

> I preached as never like to preach again,
> And as a dying man to dying men.[1]

The nature of such preaching was doctrinal and ethical, and it was assumed that the manner of the minister's life would adorn his doctrine. That is why the adultery committed by the Rev. Mr. Dimmesdale, in Hawthorne's novel, as the instructor and exemplar and saint of the theocracy, was an insult to God and the covenanted community.

Since that time preaching has often changed its character from the merely expository. With the eighteenth-century Evangelical Awakenings in America, which corresponded to the English Evangelical Revival of the same period, in which George Whitefield took a notable part in both continents, the doctrinal emphasis became subordinated to the experiential, and the rational to the emotional, and sometimes even the annals of God were neglected for the anecdotes of the preacher. In this expression of Pietism, where the essence of religion was conceived as a heart strangely warmed rather than a mind instructed by the Holy Spirit, the evangelist was born. In the time of the leaders of the Revivals, John Wesley in England and Jonathan Edwards in New England, theology and experience, a mind truly informed in Christian doctrine and a heart set on fire with the religious affections, were happily wedded. In the rough and fumbling hands of the evangelists, the knot was untied, so that light was divided from heat. The evangelists hastened to reap the fields white unto harvest with potential converts, and they were often untrained in theology, and worse, were uninterested in any theology save that crude and facile theology that produced quick results.

Up to this point a learned ministry and a relating of theology to the life of the community could be assumed. After this time Christianity and culture, theology and nurture, went their separate ways in the popular mind. For the evangelists who itinerated among the westward-moving population of America or in the rural areas and slums of England, preaching was simply an 'alarm-clock' technique, a striking for decisions, a cataclysmic 'awakening' of souls. It was, one fears, often a case of small profits and quick returns. The nadir of this type of emotional preaching with its vulgar appeals to the fear of Hell, and its crude and saccharine sentimentalism ('O, it will be, Glory for me'), was reached in the sawdust-trail appeals and the 'dynamic' chair-smashing corybantics of a Billy Sunday. The way was now open for the erotic exploitation of religion by an Aimee Semple McPherson in California. It is as an exposure of such vulgar hypocrisy that Sinclair Lewis has described the morphology of conscience in his *Elmer Gantry*, with a pathological thoroughness.

James Street, in two of his novels, *The Gauntlet* and *The High Calling*, reminds us of the importance of preaching in the average-sized church, which is never sensational in character, yet never dull. He shows that this has high instructional as well as inspirational value in the Protestant congregations stemming from the left-wing of the Reformation. It is more than a little disappointing that no significant contemporary novelist has entered fully into the difficulty of a minister in preparing sermons which shall be both theologically sound (allowing for the advance of Biblical Criticism) and relevant to the needs of the twentieth-century community.

2. Interpreters of Faith in Crisis

The next three novelists, Mrs. Humphry Ward, William Hale White (who wrote under the pseudonym of 'Mark Rutherford'), and Harold Frederic, have been selected to demonstrate ministers as interpreters of religion and culture at a time when modern science, natural and social, was making onslaughts on the traditional Christian faith. In each case, the ministers studied in these novels (an Anglican, a Congregationalist, and a Methodist) underwent agonies of skepticism, as the geology of Lyell, the biology of Darwin, and the sociology of Herbert Spencer, not to mention the radical revision of the interpretation of Christ popularized by Strauss and Renan, seemed to contradict their inherited beliefs. *Robert Elsmere*, by Mrs. Ward, recounts the crisis of faith of an Anglican rector. William Hale White gives us his own experience of religious disillusionment in *The Autobiography of Mark Rutherford*, in the course of which we learn that for him 'The dissolution of Jesus into mythologic vapour was nothing less than the death of a friend dearer to me than any other friend I ever knew.' Harold Frederic describes the shipwreck of a Methodist minister's faith and integrity as his ambition drives him to a skepticism that breaks all loyalties to his wife and his congregation. His undoing is a combination of Renanism and the 'emancipated woman.'

While the problem of correlating religious knowledge and scientific truth was felt in a peculiarly acute form in the latter part of the nineteenth century, it has not ceased to be an important issue today. It is regrettable, therefore, that this theme has not engaged twentieth-century novelists of distinction. Indeed, the task should be attempted anew in the century of Einstein and Freud.

There are other considerable gaps in the portraits of modern Protestant ministers. This is the century in which several women have been admitted to the ranks of the ministry in the so-called 'Free Churches'; yet there appears to be no significant record in modern fiction of this interesting and controversial development. Furthermore, while an important duty of the Protestant minister is to conduct public worship, there is almost no reference to this concern in the portraits of the ministry in novels. Yet here, too, there has been something of a revolution in the Evangelical Churches, many of which, especially in the United States, have responsive types of service, and some of which actually employ a liturgy.

3. Directors of Souls

It is even more curious that the Catholic novelists, with the exception of Graham Greene, who has two notable liturgical observations in *The Lawless Roads*, and Evelyn Waugh, who describes the subterfuges to which the hunted priests had to resort to celebrate the Mass in Elizabethan England in *Edmund Campion*, ignore almost entirely the liturgical responsibilities of their priests. However, it is a considerable compensation that the Catholic novelists concentrate on exploring the remarkable influence their priests have as directors of souls in and out of the confessional. The eagerness of priests to strip off the veils of false glamour with which the ugliest sins and indulgences of their penitents are covered, their insistence upon the disinfection of the ego that absolution brings, their patient and often humiliating pursuit of their spiritual charge as if he or she were the only soul in the world that God desired to restore to His fellowship, are admirably described in the novels of Bernanos and Mauriac.

There is also a remarkable difference of emphasis to be observed in the Catholic and Protestant novelists in another respect. It is that Protestants seem to rank the sins of the flesh as more heinous than the subtle and venomous sins of the spirit. For the Catholic novelists, as for the Catholic Church, the converse is true. It was particularly perceptive of Harold Frederic in *The Damnation of Theron Ware*—a novel that has received far less credit than it deserves—in comparing Protestant and Catholic conceptions of the ministry, to have observed and stressed this difference of attitude and evaluation. The pro-Catholic view is expressed by a skeptic, Dr. Ledsmar, in the words: '. . . but it seems logical to me that a church should exist for those who need its help, and not for those who by their own profession are so good already that it is they who help the church.' Other differences between the two conceptions of the ministry, such as the importance of the Sacraments, and of Penance and the Mass in particular, and the stress on celibacy are also considered in the same chapter. The chief glory of

Bernanos, Mauriac, and Greene, three Catholic novelists, is that they conceive their priests as the instruments of the Hound of Heaven.

4. Missionaries

The next group of short stories and novels are all concerned with missionaries and ministerial ambassadors of race reconciliation. As Professor Kenneth S. Latourette has shown in his monumental seven-volume *History of the Expansion of Christianity*, the period from 1800 to 1914 represented the greatest advance of missionaries in numbers, geographic spread, and influence, in the history of the Christian centuries. When it is also recognized that many of these missionaries represented the most distinguished and devoted priests and ministers of their time, it is surprising that their always sacrificial and often daunting lives have received so little attention from present-day novelists. Even more disturbing is it that such notice as they have elicited on the Protestant side has been overwhelmingly critical. The vitriolic criticism of the normally clinical Somerset Maugham in his short story *Rain* is taken under consideration largely because this has become the stereotype of the Protestant missionary in fiction. For further illumination his deep aversion to the ministry is traced in the partly autobiographical novel *Of Human Bondage*. Cronin's criticism in *Grand Canary* and his subsequent act of reparation in *The Keys of the Kingdom* shed further light on the problem. The role of the missionary in the century's most aggravatingly explosive problem, that of race relations, is studied next in Alan Paton's *Cry, the Beloved Country*.

5. Community Leaders

The newest development in the ministry and the priesthood is that which envisages them as directors of religious communities, as community leaders. In this conception of their role, they are seen performing cultural tasks, organizing, teaching, and healing, very often as a member of a team, or as its spiritual leader. In the age of specialization the minister and priest have also developed their own. The community leaders are studied in their simple origins in the Methodist minister described by Hartzell Spence in *One Foot in Heaven;* in their further elaboration in the settlement or institutional type of church through the eyes of an Episcopalian vicar in James Gould Cozzens' *Men and Brethren;* and, finally, in the most advanced conception of the community church under the leadership of a Unitarian minister depicted by Peter De Vries in *The Mackerel Plaza.*

These are not 'Edifying Discourses' in the conventional understanding of the term; but in the Kierkegaardian manner they may well suggest and provoke 'thoughts that wound from behind.' It is believed that these often critical and occasionally sympathetic studies of the ministry in modern novels cover the entire spectrum both denominationally and representatively in the realm of the fiction that can be read with pleasure and profit in the English language. The selections mirror the efforts of priests and ministers of the Roman Catholic, Anglican, Methodist, Baptist, Congregational, and Unitarian Communions. They are also a faithful mirror of what significant novelists who have written in English (or have been translated into English, in the case of Bernanos and Mauriac) have thought about the Christian religion and its official representatives in the last hundred years. To this intriguing exploration the ensuing chapters are devoted.

II

Preachers and Evangelists

IT was a man and a poet who had suffered much from the inquisitorial ministers of the Presbyterian Church of Scotland, Robert Burns, who cried:

> O wad some Pow'r the giftie gie us
> To see ourselves as others see us!
> It wad frae mony a blunder free us,
>   And foolish notion.

Ministers, even more than the rest of men, need such mirrors. But where are they to be found? In their wives? But the mirror is misted over with affection when the lady of the manse looks at him. Would their congregations provide a truer reflection? Even here, distortion is more likely than true reflection; for the admirers of the minister hold out the golden mirror of adulation, in which he is only too ready to recognize the idealized version of himself; and the critics in the congregation either steal silently away to another congregation or so enrage him with their exaggerations that what he sees in the mirror is the distorted lineaments of his torturers, not his own impassioned image.

To be sure, there will be distortions as well as true reflections. But the distortions may serve to point out the peculiar temptations of the vocation, whether these be pomposity, snobbishness,

21

complacency, conventionalism, the trite answer to a profound question (the sin in the Vicar of Blackstable that Somerset Maugham's character Philip was unable to forgive), and, above all, conformity to the world in its social values and its groveling worship of success. Hypocrisy may take these and a myriad other Protean forms, which the critical novelist can unveil.

There will also be sympathetic portraits, which will serve as encouragements in a profession dedicated to sacrifice, which receives many tokens of affection, but aptly not the highest in a materialistic world. Such portrayals will be further inducements to the life of charity in a world of cheap sarcasms and character assassination, to the stimulation of that forgiveness that mends embittered relationships, to the increase of that compassion which always runs the second mile in helpfulness, to the openness which looks for the best in every human being, to the humility and modesty that a brash and arrogant era needs, and, finally, to that steady submission to the rule of God with the assistance of Divine grace that brings contentment and direction to the mad, dissatisfied, frenetic moderns.

The novels which provide the mirrors of the ministry in this chapter will be more meaningfully studied if it is realized that they represent two variations of the historic Protestant ministry. Historically, the Protestant minister was first the Minister of the Word of God, his chief function being to proclaim the Revelation of the living God as recorded in the sacred oracles of the Scriptures for the edification of souls. In Colonial America in the early days of the Puritan theocracy, of which Hawthorne writes, the minister was primarily the preacher but he was also the moral leader and exemplar of his community. A learned and scholarly ministry is still the aim and ideal of the Puritan tradition, whether in the Congregational, the Presbyterian, or the Low Anglican ministry. With the coming of the Pietistic movement of the eighteenth century, however, a new

race of Christian leaders came into being:—the Evangelists; and
it is with this second type of ministry that Sinclair Lewis deals in
Elmer Gantry. The stress is less on the doctrinal element and
more on the experiential, less on the Christian as a member of
the religio-political community and more on him as a saved soul.
The Dissenting conception of a 'gathered church' in England
and the post-Revolutionary separation of Church and State
in America led to a voluntary pluralism of congregations, thus
forcing every minister to become to some degree an evangelist
to increase his congregation. In the nineteenth century in the
United States the rapid westward moving of the frontier, the
depopulation of the rural areas caused by increasing industrialization, and the continuing influx of immigrants, made the
itinerating evangelist and pastor the second type of the ministry
in America. These conditions will be reflected to some degree
in the three novelists now under consideration: Nathaniel
Hawthorne, Sinclair Lewis, and James Street.

Hawthorne provides a lively account of a State-supported
Congregational and Calvinistic minister of the Word, the leader
of a Puritan theocracy, in his *Scarlet Letter* (1850). Sinclair
Lewis in *Elmer Gantry* (1927) portrays an itinerant evangelist
whose pragmatism eventually finds the best outlet in Methodism. In *The God-Seeker* (1949) the same author delineates a
nineteenth-century boy leaving his New England and Congregational home to become a missionary to the Sioux Indians in
the central plains under the aegis of the American Board of
Commissioners for Foreign Missions. James Street, first in *The
Gauntlet* (1945) and then in its continuation *The High Calling*
(1951), describes the life of the young and the maturing London Wingo, a Southern Baptist minister, as he practices his profession in Missouri, dependent entirely upon the financial support of his congregations.

1. Hawthorne

The Scarlet Letter is America's first great novel and it was
written in the great introspective Puritan tradition. Taking the
seventeenth-century symbol for marital infidelity, the cruel
scarlet letter 'A' an adulteress was required to wear to adver-
tise abroad her inner frailty and shame, he traced the subtle,
diverse, and protracted effects of human sin. What the characters are within is exteriorized in most dramatic fashion. Hester,
despite her badge of shame, glows with serenity, thus proving
that a spiritual enrichment has ensued from her humble
acceptance of her sin's consequences and her genuine penitence.
Dimmesdale, the erring minister, grows more pallid daily as
his remorse seems to eat him away. The evil desiccation of the
heart through neglect, at the expense of the diabolical cultiva-
tion of the intelligence in Chillingworth, Hester's husband,
makes him disintegrate before our eyes, as he grows visibly more
wizened at each appearance. The moral of the story is found
in its most uncomplicated form in the comment of little Pearl,
Dimmesdale's natural daughter, as she meets her father in the
open woods, and exclaims in the profound silence: 'Thou wast
not bold! Thou wast not true!' In brief, Hawthorne's novel is
the parable of the failure of a most promising ministry because
of lack of integrity and because of timidity. It is also an epitaph
for Puritanism, written two centuries after the days of its greatest glories.

Hawthorne confronts his Puritan Congregational ancestors
with both fascination and repulsion. He is intrigued by their
concern for the inner life of man and their profound determination to serve God in every aspect of life, political and vocational,
as well as ecclesiastical. He is also fascinated by their doctrine
of particular providences by which they attribute all happen-

ings to primary causes, whether divine or demonic, even though this has become in a scientific age a matter of less moment. He is, however, deeply disgusted and repelled by the hypocrisy that made the public faces so different from the private lives of so many Puritan officials. He is entirely out of sympathy with the unmerciful and unforgiving Calvinistic Deity, who is justice, and even an arbitrary type of justice who seems to sanction vengefulness in human affairs. He finds peculiarly appalling the hard legalism of most of this God's devotees in the ministry and the magistracy. His chief concern, however, is with the moral paradox that it is only through the experience of frailty that independence and sympathy grow. Only thus can the chains of convention be broken, even though they almost break the individual in the process. Like a Rembrandt painting in chiaroscuro, his characters are neither wholly black nor wholly white, but gray symbols of the moral life: becoming blacker like Chillingworth or whiter like Hester.

The minister, Dimmesdale, is the third figure in importance in the novel. Hester is the most dominant, courageous in her truthfulness but never entirely honest; then the demonic doctor, Chillingworth. The minister, Dimmesdale, is presented as a man of brilliant parts, profound sympathy, and great erudition, who yet has the fatal flaw of hypocrisy. He is profoundly sensitive, and is literally eaten away by remorse through hiding his collusion in the act of adultery with Hester.

Why did Hawthorne choose a minister for this role? Partly because the moral leader of the community would best show the nature of hypocrisy and the fatal flaw of Puritanism; partly also because of the unrivaled position of a seventeenth-century minister in New England as an exponent of the inner life so dear to the theocracy. His temptation to hide his sin was the greater because of the great public confidence in him; his hypocrisy was the greater in that he was God's plenipotentiary and

viceregent in the eyes of the parish, a blameless servant of God
whose asceticism and spiritual ardors and self-inflicted penances
were believed to be bringing on an untimely death.

Thus Hawthorne describes his role and underlines the temptation to enter this vocation for the wrong reason:

Next in order to the magistrates came the young and eminently distinguished divines, from whose lips the religious discourse of the anniversary [the Election Sermon] was expected. His was the profession, at
that era, in which intellectual ability displayed itself far more than in
political life; for—leaving a higher motive out of the question—it offered
inducements powerful enough, in the almost worshipping respect of the
community, to win the most aspiring ambition into its service. Even
political power—as in the case of Increase Mather—was within the grasp
of a successful priest.[1]

The cult of popularity—is this less insidious today for the modern minister? Probably the reputation for erudition is today
no recommendation for a minister in most pulpits, but the reputation for integrity is still a paramount need and expectation.

Dimmesdale's type, that of the intellectual and sensitive mystic of astonishing eloquence and sanctity, was by no means the
only one among the New England ministry, says Hawthorne,
who knew his history well as a thorough antiquarian. There
were more remarkable scholars than Dimmesdale; there were
men endowed 'with a far greater share of shrewd, hard, iron,
and granite understanding; which, mingled with a fair proportion of doctrinal ingredient, constitutes a highly efficacious, and
unamiable variety of the clerical species.'[2] Again, there were
saintlier men than Dimmesdale. But they all lacked the fire of
eloquence, the gift of immediate communication in the heart's
native language.

Dimmesdale would naturally have belonged to the latter type.

To the high mountain peaks of faith and sanctity he would have climbed, had not the tendency been thwarted by the burden . . . beneath which it was his doom to totter. It kept him down to a level with the lowest; this very burden it was gave him sympathies so intimate with the sinful brotherhood of mankind, so that his heart vibrated in unison with theirs, and received their pain into itself, and sent its throb of pain through a thousand hearts, in gushes of sad, persuasive eloquence. Oftenest persuasive, but sometimes terrible! [3]

Hawthorne raises the important question: What was and still is the charm of religious orthodoxy? The Transcendentalist answers:

Mr. Dimmesdale was a true priest, a true religionist, with the reverential sentiment largely developed, and an order of mind that impelled itself powerfully along the track of a creed, and wore its passage continually deeper with the lapse of time. In no state of society would he have been what is called a man of liberal views; it would always be essential to his peace to feel the pressure of a faith about him, supporting, while it confined him within its iron framework. [4]

(Hawthorne contrasts the immense depth and range of Chillingworth's ideas with the paucity of Dimmesdale's convictions.)

What, then, are the conclusions that Hawthorne would wish his readers to draw from his illuminating narrative? The conclusion which we are to draw from the minister's life is this: 'Among many morals which press upon us from the poor minister's experience, we put only this into a sentence: "Be true! Be true! Be true! Show freely to the world, if not your worst, some trait whereby the worst may be inferred!" ' In similar fashion, from Hester's woe and penitence, he would teach us that the wounded are the best counsellors, and that sacred love alone warrants the great passion. From Chillingworth's life we are to learn that utter dedication to the intellect can lead to the atrophy and desiccation of the heart. Furthermore, from Puritanism we are to learn the blindness of Pharisaism (Mauriac will teach the same lesson) and moral rigorism. This lack of the creative capacity for compassion is itself dependent upon a recognition of universal frailty and on the need of a continually renewed Divine forgiveness. We are also to know that the doctrine of Election is a peculiar comfort to Pharisees, even though it limits the love of God by an arbitrary justice. Above all we are warned that there is an infinite distance between Divine Judgment and human justice. But Puritanism also had its great qualities: its sense of the importance of the learned ministry, utilizing reason and scholarship for the glory of God, from John Cotton to Jonathan Edwards; its insistence that sanctification is the correlate and conclusion of justification. But the greatest flaw in any ministry is hypocrisy.

2. *Sinclair Lewis*

Sinclair Lewis maintains the same viewpoint in his scathing description of the arch-hypocrite *Elmer Gantry*. His theme is the ruthless exploitation of religion for self-aggrandizement as expressed in the soiled life of Elmer Gantry through a variety of compromises. The notorious Elmer is first a Baptist minister, then a traveling representative (was he really ever anything else but the man who advertised himself?), then the chief assistant of a glamorous woman evangelist, then an independent evangelist himself, then an assistant to a woman leader of 'New Thought,' and finally a pragmatically sensationalist Methodist minister with ambitions for heading a National Society for the Purity of Art and the Press.

Elmer's native abilities are two: a gift of gab and the extrovert's equipment:—a roaring voice and a back-slapping manner. Lewis says: 'He was born to be a Senator. He never said anything important and he always said it sonorously. He could make "Good Morning" seem as profound as Kant, welcoming as a brass-band, and uplifting as a cathedral organ. It was a 'cello his voice, and in the enchantment of it you did not hear his slang, his boasting, his smut, and the dreadful violence which (at this period) he performed on singulars and plurals.'[5] He would have been happy in the prize-ring, the stock-exchange, or the fishmarket. He is a back-slapping bully and, of course, a coward. He is introduced in a drunkenly belligerent mood, the muscular football captain of a zealous Baptist-related college in Kansas.

So unlikely a candidate for the ministry must get into it by accident. And he did. He fights some free-thinking men in a neighboring town who have challenged a weedy classmate's right to preach the Gospel in the open. This zeal for pugnacity for its own sake, however, is interpreted as the repentance of a Christian soldier.

The conversion, when it comes, must be skin deep, because so was the narrow and superficial Christian culture he had imbibed. Religion was taught to him as a series of melodramatic possibilities and sentimentalities. Adolescent Elmer hears of the ship's captain in the storm saved by the prayer of an orphan child; the tale of a little lame Tom who shamed the wicked rich man who owned the team of grays and pot hat and led him to Jesus; and, also, of the faithful dog who saved his master from a fire and thus roused him to give up one trinity of delights— horse-racing, rum, and the harmonica,—for the Holy Trinity. This was the staple diet of his Sunday School teaching in the Baptist Church of Paris, Kansas. 'The Church, the Sunday School, the evangelistic orgy, choir practice, raising the mortgage, the delights of funerals, the snickers in back pews or in the other room at weddings—they were as natural, as inescapable a mold of manners to Elmer as Catholic processionals to a street gamin in Naples!'[6] The weaknesses of pietism, without its strength made Elmer Gantry. There was no correlation of religion with reason, none with decency, and little enough with kindness. Even if these had existed, he was too egotistical for such Christian medicaments to take!

He had no friends, but even his associates were not very helpful. The outstanding Christian on campus was Eddie Fislinger, a Baptist local preacher, a Y.M.C.A. Christian, a weed but a Christian weed. 'Whatever difficulties he may have had with Latin and calculus, there had never been a time since the age of twelve when Eddie Fislinger had had difficulty in understanding what the Lord Almighty wanted, and why, all through history, He had acted thus or thus.'[7] This narrow dogmatist knew all the answers and was not at a loss to provide slick answers to all deep problems or the necessary stereotype of either 'conversion' or the 'call' to the ministry. Eddie's word for annihilating the attacks of Higher Criticism was simple and effective: 'It's better to have a whole Bible than a Bible full of holes.'[8]

Judson Roberts, the State Secretary of the Y.M.C.A., was no help either. The muscularity of this ex-University of Chicago football hero had to stand in for mentality. Lewis sketches him clearly: 'Big as a grizzly, jolly as a spaniel pup, radiant as ten suns.'[9] He was slangy, slick, in well with God and the fraternities. In fact, a real, red-blooded, regular fellow. He simply desired the unchanged or superficially changed Elmer to jump on to the conversion band-wagon and play the part of a decoy statistic on the campus. Not surprisingly, then, Elmer's 'conversion' was due to crowd pressure. First, there were hymns of a sentimental, folksy kind to break down his resistance; his mother was brought in to sit beside the boy convert-to-be; his converted team-mates and even the College President pleaded in an orgy of emotionalism for this Very Important Young Man to enter the kingdom. Could he help it if he thought he was conferring an honor on the ministry? Finally, Roberts, the great he-man, the complete athlete removed the possibility of the reproach of Christianity's being a 'sissy's' calling, when he preached on the text 'rejoiceth as a strong man to run a race.'

How could a young man as irresponsible and nearly illiterate as Elmer Gantry think of entering the ministry? In his befuddled brain, there were four stages, or should we call them 'slithers,' into it? First, by the process of elimination his desire to become a lawyer faded with the recognition that even the gift of gab would not prevail with a jury over a smarter legal opponent. Secondly, community pressure and the flattery of president, professors, and students took its toll. Thirdly, he soon saw in the ministry a quick way to become a public figure, without the slightest ethical transformation. St. Augustine may have prayed, 'O God, make me chaste but not yet'—but Elmer improved on this: 'O God make me chaste, but not in this life.' Finally, the desired call came in a fantastic way. Even Elmer could not stand the pressure of the combined operations of the faculty in a marathon prayer-meeting for him. He escaped in the middle of it, sought refuge in an overdose of straight whiskies, and deceived the faculty, with the aid of peppermints to sweeten his sour breath, and himself into believing because all was well in his bemused soul, God was in his heaven and all's right with Elmer. Thus it was that this hypocrite received his call. It was ironically just that the deceiver was self-deceived, even if it strains our credulity overmuch to believe that the Bible belt snoopers could not detect that this 'call' came from distilled spirits, not from the Holy Spirit.

The Seminary, at which he spent three years, merely sharpened his shrewdness without deepening his spirituality. He picked up confidence in elocution, an impressive vocabulary, and a pretentious smattering of learned languages. Lewis says 'Although he had almost flunked in Greek, his thesis on "Six-

teen Ways of Paying a Church Debt" had won the ten-dollar
prize in Practical Theology.'[10]

His tricks, they do not warrant the description of techniques,
are illuminating as a piece of skulduggery. First, he used poly-
syllables to impress country folk with his extraordinary learning. Then, he was not hampered in his imagination by any regard for the truth. For example, he always lied about his fond-
ness for the seminary faculty, whom he loathed. When he got
into the ministry he did not allow his independence to be
tramelled by any sense of professional loyalty to his colleagues.
Thirdly, his flock was used as a mere sounding-board for his
preaching personality. He referred to the folk at his first church
as 'a group of hicks.' Fourthly, his sermons relate imaginary anecdotes for edifying purposes as if they were sober truths of
his own experience. With the retelling they grow more glutin-
ous and more improbable. Fifthly, all honest doubt was always
to be discouraged and never met; hence honest religion was
quite unthinkable for him. Sixthly, he was without scruple in
making insinuations of others, whether his seniors or contemporaries: he reported to the Dean of the Seminary that Dr.
Bruno Zechlin, a Dutch scholar of great learning and liberal
views, was an infidel and a socialist. The result was that this
good man was immediately fired and died two years later. Years
later he was to betray his former friend and associate minister,
Frank Shallard, simply to wean away from Shallard's church
a wealthy millionaire and capture him for his own church.

Such a man, who will use everyone for his own ends, will not
be reluctant to exploit the hunger of men and provide them instead of bread with a diet even more superficial than the prodigal's husks. Lewis gives a brilliant discussion of revivalist
techniques in Chapter XIV, in which he shows the mercenari-
ness of the approach, the playing on the emotions, the faking
of the statistics, and the use of the converts and local ministers

for the glorification and greed of the evangelists. It is not surprising that Gantry was an apt pupil of Rose Falconer, the glamorous lady evangelist whose assistant and lover he became.

When accepted for the Methodist ministry, Gantry made the city hum with his 'Lively Sunday Evenings.' They were the last word in advertising and self-service. 'Once to illustrate the evils of betting, he had them bet as to which of two frogs would jump first. Once he had the representative of an illustrious grape-juice company hand around sample glasses of his beverage to illustrate the superiority of soft drinks to the horrors of alcohol. And once he had up on the platform a sickening twisted motor-car in which three people had been killed at a railroad crossing. With this as an example, he showed his flock that speeding was but one symptom of the growing madness and worldliness and materialism of the age, and that this madness could be cured only by turning to the simple old-time religion as preached in the Wellspring Methodist Church' in Zenith, Winnemac.[11]

His most successful line was prurience—that is, by attacks on vice which attracted the fearful who could eradicate vice by proxy and be stimulated at the same time. Elmer was an expert at making the worst of two worlds seem like the best. His chief exploit in this phase of his life was to wear the uniform of a lieutenant of police and to lead a police raid on the dens of vice —the red-light rooms and the liquor saloons. His only accomplishment was to embarrass a poor wasted female made desperate by poverty.

Sensationalism creates the demand for more sensationalism, and while his stunts lasted the people flocked to the doors of his church for titillation not truth. 'Every Sunday night now people were turned from the doors of Elmer's Church. If they did not always have a sermon about vice, at least they enjoyed the saxophone solos, and singing, "There'll be a Hot Time in the Old Town Tonight." And once they were entertained by a professional juggler who wore (it was Elmer's own idea) a placard proclaiming that he stood for "God's Word" and who showed how easy it was to pick up weights symbolically labelled "Sin" and "Sorrow" and "Ignorance" and "Papistry." '[12]

By contrast with the lascivious, lying, sanctimonious evangelist and minister that Gantry is, Lewis paints miniatures of two good ministers. It is, however, significant that they are not successful. One of them is old 'father' Andrew Pengilly, a Methodist mystic, and the other the honest and self-critical liberal Frank Shallard, who finds first the Baptists and then the Congregationalists too traditional and finally crusades for liberalism at the time of the Dayton trial. The only result of his gentle crusade is that a gang of Literalist thugs trick him into entering a car, bind him, thrash and whip him within an inch of his life, and leave his right eye mere blinded pulp. Obviously, for Sinclair Lewis, honest religion or a truly compassionate ministry are contradictions in terms. Neither the ministry nor the churches are interested in the rational, the tolerant, the generous, the humble, or the humane. Christians who hold such convictions are dreary or dramatic failures, doomed men. It is the self-deceived and emotionally deceiving, the pious humbugs, the stunters, the ruthlessly ambitious, back-slapping, and thigh-tickling men like Elmer Gantry who succeed. It is a sorry verdict on the ministry and the churches, if a tenth of the contention be true. But, true or not, *Elmer Gantry* is a formidable warning against hypocrisy, the cult of personality in the pulpit, and the temptations of mere elocution, and the dangers of a skin-deep and narrow Christian culture and education. It is for every individual reader to determine whether this is a portrait or a caricature, a scarecrow or a case of 'There but for the grace of God go I.'

Lewis himself knew how much he had scandalized the conventional churchgoer by this portrait of a minister. For myself, I believe that his second endeavor with a clerical character, twenty-two years later, was an attempt at correcting an exaggeration, an act of reparation, if you will. In the fifth chapter of this book it will be suggested that A. J. Cronin also wanted a second chance to do a better job of describing the Protestant missionary. The *amende honorable* for *Grand Canary* was the picture of the American Methodist medical missionary who is friendly with the Scottish priest and hero of *The Keys of the Kingdom.* Sinclair Lewis' act of reparation for *Elmer Gantry* is found in *The God-Seeker.* He is not converted in the interval, as Cronin was, but he has a respect for his hero in *The God-Seeker,* whereas he had only contempt for mendacious Elmer Gantry.

The theme of *The God-Seeker* is the search for ideals by which to live on the part of Aaron Gadd, a carpenter of the Berkshire hills in Massachusetts, who was converted by a subordinate of Charles Finney the evangelist, and decided to become a missionary to the Indians under the American Board of Commissioners for Foreign Missions. He lost his Calvinism in time but retained his humanitarianism, becoming first a Unitarian and finally a Socialist, if a well-heeled one, in the pioneer days of St. Paul, Minnesota. In this novel the ministry is not consciously hypocritical, merely deluded. And the most honest of them sees that what he always admired in the Gospel of the carpenter of Nazareth was the socialism. Sinclair Lewis is as much a propagandist as any preacher.

There are several clerical characters in this novel. Harge, an ex-lawyer, always dilating on the financial sacrifice he has made to become a missionary, yet so impractical as to give grave doubt as to whether he could manage an office far less the mission station of which he is chief. He is a rhetorician, a man of short breath, and excessively uxorious. He is rather pathetically unsuccessful in his attempt to convert Indians. His chief colleague at the mission station is the learned but useless Congregational minister, Mr. Speezer, who for his present task might have benefited more from a farmyard than from Harvard Yard. He has a library of seventy books and is mad on Plato and Patristics! Finney makes a brief and dramatic appearance, but his eloquence lacks the distinctive gift of the real Finney, his uncanny lawyer's ability to divine the motives of human actions. There are also two other odd clergy—one an abolitionist Unitarian, Euripides Tattam, and the other a homosexual mystical masochist from Nashotah who brings up the High Episcopalian rear of the procession. It seems that the more heterodox the theology, the more delighted Lewis is with his characters.

The chief character, Aaron Gadd, is an honest carpenter, sincere, courageous, and sensible, if uneducated. Lewis gives us an unforgettable picture of an ornery old-time New England layman, which type has not yet entirely died out, whose ruthless and granite honesty has a strong appeal. He is a vigorous dying grandfather and he sees Aaron, his grandson, for the first time, when the boy is taken on a visit with his harsh father, a deacon, and the Congregational minister. The deacon introduces his son, after the query, 'This your spawn?'

'This is Aaron, my youngest—ten now.'

'Don't look it. Too handsome and too blame cheerful to be any of your stale leavin's. And who,' he indicated the benevolent Mr. Fairlow, 'who the hell may this pickle-face be?'

'Now, Dad, you know well this is Reverend Fairlow, my pastor.'

'Is, is he? Board of deacons never look into his morals? He looks to me like a widow-tickler. Bet he steals sermons out of Cotton Mather. Never trust these Miss Nancy's with silky mustaches.'

The poor Reverend pleaded, 'Now, Daddy Gadd.'

'Not *your* daddy, thank God—or don't think so!'

Mr. Fairlow tried again: 'Well, Captain, we've come in all tenderness and loving faith in God to ask you to pray for us before it be too late.'

'Nope. Done my own prayin' since I was two year old. Calc'late to go right on. God and me been good friends eighty-five years now, old friends, and we don't like you slick young squirts rampagin' in and interruptin' two old gentlemen when they're talking theology. God is still mighty puzzled about the combination of determinism and the efficacy of his grace, but we're tryin' out a scheme that we want to talk out with Brahma and Zoroaster, and we don't want you apprentices disturbin' us.'

Fairlow was convinced that Satan was speaking through the grandfather's lips. Daddy Gadd dismisses the two men with the information that he has left the Congregational fold

'and this mornin' I done a job of thinkin' and I wrassled Hell and threw it and was minded to quit the Episcopalians too. I sent for the Universalist preacher up here and kind of informally joined his church—in fact, took over his finances and told him how to raise the mortgage on that cow-brindle shanty he calls a church.'

'He was like you boys,' he adds, 'wanted to give me a letter of recommendation to the Almighty, because while the Universalists know there ain't any fiery hell, they still get suspicious of that smell of smoke. But I told him if my old friend God wanted me—which ain't any too certain —God would recognize me after eighty-five years without any secretary or hired man, like you boys, remindin' him who I be.'[13]

The dignity, simplicity, courage, and fierce independence of the old man are, so the novelist implies, inherited by his grandson, who finds it necessary to shake off the dust of his father's farm after the latter's exhibition of unnecessary vindictiveness toward his dog in which he kills the beast. This hero is at least honest, says Lewis.

Lewis has a fascinating study in mixed motives in the appeal which Harge, one of Finney's henchmen drumming up missionary recruits, makes successfully to young Aaron Gadd, within half an hour of his conversion in a crowd. First Harge ap-

peals to the lure of adventure in the unknown West. 'Your heart
would be wrung if you could see how critical for all future time
is our work among the Sioux—or the Dakotas, as they presume
to call themselves. They are clotted with evil.' With this is
mixed an appeal to save them and gain glory in the world to
come. Harge's second tactic is to appeal to the novelty of the
new life and the dire need of the Indians—again a mixed approach. 'And those grand prairies, millions of acres, right up
to the bastions of the Rocky mountains; buffalo and bear and
beaver; riding wild horses—not stick here, wedged into a village!' Then a cry from the heart for perishing Indian souls.
Aaron shudders at the thought of perishing Indians, 'That would
be bad. I wish I were a minister and had the training...' Now the
wily old fisherman has him on the hook, and the bait is both
spiritual and material, as before. 'You come with us, Aaron and
you'll get it free. Mr. Speezer, my collaborator, and I will instruct you in theology, Greek, everything! Also, both of us
speak and preach in Sioux—to some extent. You shall study under the best conditions, free from temptations. What we need is
a pure young man who's a blame good farmer and builder, and in
return we'll give you of our learning.' In fact, they make him
their cheap artificer and he gets hardly a modicum of the little
learning they have to give. Aaron reaches the appropriately
named 'Forest of the Dead' mission (Bois des Morts) to find it
not so much a one-horse town as a one-cow garbage heap.

Lewis makes much of the contrast between expectation and
realization. Harge makes the introductions:

Then there stalked in, very pleasant, altogether high-class, somewhat
as though they were slumming but didn't mind, the Reverend Herbert
Henry Speezer, M.A., and Luna Davenport Speezer. He was bald and
whiskerless, dry, sparkling, scholarly, lightly humorous; she, thin, ener-
getic, hawklike and (considering a missionary's salary) elegant, with
black jet earrings.... [Speezer then held Aaron's hand, as he breathed,]

Mr. Gadd, you cannot possibly know how fortunate we deem ourselves in having a new companion who may constitute a new audience for our little jokes and eschatological theories! We shall do everything we can to make you happy and ... *where's the supplies, Squire?* [14]

Evidently, they were more interested in what Aaron had brought than in the young man himself. In actual fact, the supplies consisted of new satinet pantaloons, flannel chest-protectors, and, most excitingly, Locke's *Human Understanding* and Epictetus in Greek! Lewis has no time for pedants, less time than the Indians had, one would guess.

Sinclair Lewis gives us no obvious moral, but one may be found in the chuckling agnosticism which is expressed by Black Wolf, the Oberlin-educated Indian, who despises the missionaries for their naïvete. He turns out to be not an Indian Tom Paine, but just a little Tom twinge! He has prepared a learned pamphlet, entitled 'Religion and Superstition.' Here is his view of the white man's religion:

Most of the whites believe, or profess to believe in Christianity, which is an idolatrous religion with many gods. Their Catholic sect has thousands of mysterious divine beings ruled by what they call the 'Trinity,' which consists of Father, Son, and Mother Mary. The Protestants have no Trinity, but a four-god council consisting of Father, Son, Holy Ghost, and Satan. . . . Among their demi-gods are Santa Claus, Luck (whom they worship by striking wood), saints, angels, seraphs, witches, fairies, vampires, evil spirits, the spirits of the dead, tombs and statues, the cross and a magic book called the Bible. [15]

Though nowhere explicit, his view seems to be that Christianity is an illusion, but one which generates a morality of compassion and social reform. There is a minimum of supernaturalism and theology in Unitarianism, and a maximum of social reform, so that is the best form of the delusion. An honest man's the noblest work of God, and honest men come out of the chrysalis of the outworn skin of Christian superstition and fly their wings as free men dedicated to the welfare of the community. The view is a common one—it seems to be very much the view that Somerset Maugham is expounding in his autobiographical *Of Human Bondage*, except that for Lewis's socialism we must substitute Maugham's compassion and tolerance.

Has this volume, *The God-Seeker*, any particular message for the ministry? Throughout there is implicit a plea for honest religion instead of mixed motives and windy rhetoric. But the cutting edge is a concern that the practical effect of a genuine Christianity be shown in a regeneration of the social order, through the expression of social justice. And that appeal—as its counterfeit in Communism shows—has not lost any of its relevance, and it is the Gospel of the Incarnation that is the only adequate lever for providing such a transformation. Sinclair Lewis's exaggerations should not blind us to this truth.

3. James Street

James Street, a former Baptist minister, has written the most recent and sympathetic account of the Protestant ministry in the mid-West in his two novels about London Wingo, the first entitled *The Gauntlet*, (1945) and the second, *The High Calling* (1951).[16] Rather than profound interpretations of the nature of the ministry in the twentieth century, or even critiques, they are the faithful documentaries of the drudgery and some of the glory of the men who have to run the gauntlet in maintaining their high calling. They will not detain us as long as our previous novels.

His chief value to ministers (he has also an important interpretative role for laymen) is the sympathy with which he elaborates the problems of the modern Protestant pastor in America. These he views in personal concrete terms which make them vivid, but also over-simplify them. Moreover, some of the more complex and subtle social problems to be faced by the churches, such as race relations or the communication of the gospel to a rootless society in a mechanistic age, are either not touched upon or dismissed too rapidly. With these limitations, however, his work is important and rewarding.

Street's chief concern is with a double problem: How is the minister to preserve his intellectual integrity and his personal and family life against the pressures of his congregation? London Wingo, his hero, has to run the gauntlet, as a young Baptist minister straight out of the seminary. While religion satisfies his emotional needs it has not yet gripped his mind with conviction. To his simple but profoundly believing friend, Musselwhite, he says: 'I want to find Truth. It seems to me that at times, my mind, my reason, is challenging my spirit, throwing down a gauntlet and daring my spirit to pick it up.' Page makes the rather obvious reply that it's simply a matter of finding God. 'But sometimes,' London said, 'the whole thing doesn't make sense. God and the myths and the inconsistencies. I find myself thinking that maybe man invented God to cover up his own ignorance, that man is God's ego because man must think of himself as a special animal.'[17]

His quest for truth makes him veer toward modernism and humanism in reaction to the obscurantism that often passes for religion in the Bible-belt. He is clearly impressed, perhaps over-impressed by the Biblical Higher Criticism, to the point where he prefaces his readings with a parade of modern hypotheses. But there is also a deeper problem which, he admits to his wife, he is shirking.

I don't dare tell my church that religion is nothing except humanity; that the God who sent bears to eat little children because they laughed at a bald-headed man never existed except in the superstitions and myths of nomadic savages, and in the fairy tales of a few lecherous grasping old men who were determined to control and deceive the people.[18]

His oversimplified creed is that 'Religion is humanity and Jesus is love, and that's all there is to it.' At the same time he acknowledges that people don't want the truth because it is too simple. 'They want the privilege of hate without losing the luxury of love.' In his utter despair he thinks of quitting the ministry, so humanist does he become. His wife insists that only Christian humanism, not the stoicism of Ingersoll's brand, will benefit the common people. We are given no clue as to how he solves intellectual problems, except that they become less urgent; he becomes more disciplined and humble, and the resurrection becomes an existential concern for him with the death of his wife in the birth of their second child, a stillborn son, with which the book closes. Such fideism is not really the answer to a problem that is posed in intellectual, not moral terms.

The second part of the problem is common to all ministers and their wives. It is the goldfish bowl existence, which makes private life practically impossible, and the powerful pressures on both from the congregation to conform rather than be themselves! In the development of this problem, Street is really at his best and his most amusing. Allied with it is Wingo's own problem of insisting on his independence and refusing to knuckle down before the deacons, and yet not to become truculent and arrogant himself. The deacons will insist on thinking that he is their employee, not the servant of the living God. Street manages to make one see in the bitter controversy between the parsonage and the diaconate that there is truth on both sides of the fence, even if the deacons' side seems more darkly sinister. The author certainly has no time for the two dominating deacons' wives who are the Pharisees of the story. He uses three symbols to exploit to the full the church's invasion of the legitimate privacy of the parsonage. The first is 'Jezzy,' short for Jezebel, their name for a dull bronze replica of the winged victory of Samothrace, which has to serve as a lamp stand, given Wingo and Kathie by the women of the Church, and which they loathe. This they hide under the sofa and re-establish in its place whenever a church member appears at the door. When Wingo ceases to perform this minor act of church rebellion, Kathie feels that he is already being beaten into conformism.

The second symbol is what they call the yellow peril, something between a pillow and a cushion. This has been made by the woman's association and it is signed with the names of all the women members of two years' standing—the limitation is to keep out a special friend of the minister's wife who joined less than a year before. One of the female Pharisees insists that it must be placed on the love-seat which Kathie brought back from the family home to displace the appalling red sofa that the church had given them. The pillow-cushion is the reassertion of the church's rights in the parsonage—and therefore an object of ministerial disgust. A crisis is precipitated when the leading Pharisee visits unexpectedly and asks where the object is. It has been hidden beneath dirty rags in the linen cupboard, and the daughter of the parsonage drags it out into the light of day. The Pharisee interprets this as a symbol of the ingratitude of the parsonage, and the fur and feathers fly.

The third symbol is the determination of the Pharisees that Kathie shall always be referred to as Katherine, as being more dignified for a minister's wife than the diminutive. The combined effect of these symbols is to show the unrelieved pressure of the women members of the Baptist congregation to cramp the gaiety and spontaneity of a woman who was remarkable in mingling a sound faith with joyousness.

The trouble between the deacons' wives and the minister's wife is an image of the constant fight between the deacons and the pulpit. The dilemma the minister has to face is always the relative claims of truth and tact, because he has to persuade, not dictate to, his people. This, indeed, poses a problem for the conscientious minister. Can he actually include the serpent's wisdom with the dove's innocence and not impair his integrity?

The most disturbing feature of *The Gauntlet* comes exactly at this point. Street seems to admire the shrewdness of the minister who tells 'white lies' and works by devious indirection. But however necessary compromises may be in politics, they seem to me to be betrayals in the redeemed community, the church of Christ. Street shows us Honeycutt, the retiring minister helping Wingo's candidature by telling the deacons after they have heard Wingo preach that another church is interested in him, when this is absolutely untrue. This may be good psychology, but it is intolerable Christian ethics. It is also a shallow defense of Honeycutt's conscience for him to say jocularly to Wingo that he has not been informed that the statement is untrue, for he has not been informed that it *is* true!

The same approach by indirection is used to stir up local competition between towns to have a local hospital built, and Wingo even arranges for his wife to go to the next town's hospital to have a baby, by getting her doctor to perjure himself by saying that there may be complications which would make it inadvisable to have her baby at home. This so enrages the local community that in their inferiority complex they start busily raising a building fund for their own hospital. The same old capitalistic and competitive trick is employed by London Wingo and his friend the Baptist minister in the neighboring town, acting as conspirators unknown to their people to build new churches and parsonages from local rivalry. This seems to me to be a species of Protestant Jesuitry—the end justifying the means. The author, more sophisticated than I, regards such ruses as only 'a fib for the Lord.'[19] If this is the only way a minister can survive in the modern Protestant church—and I

would like to know if this is so—then the caricatures of Sinclair
Lewis may be nearer the truth than one suspects.

Perhaps the most dramatic part of the novel shows the minister in an act of outstanding courage, when he officiates at a new
kind of shot-gun wedding, where the unconsenting father of
the bride oiled his shot-gun for the preacher! Here was indeed
a dilemma. In Kathie's eyes it could be stated thus: 'If you don't
marry them your own people will say that you are a coward.
If you do, that old Newt Upjohn may try to kill you. Brotherly
love! Good lord, what mockery, what ignorance!' The wedding is performed and Wingo, fearing death, steels himself to
inform the trigger-happy father of the fact. The latter con-
temptuously turns his back on the minister. But the final act of
courage on Wingo's part—the proof that he has run the gauntlet—is to decide to stay on in his church, despite his wife's death,
the invitation to accept a wealthy suburban congregation, and
the maltreatment he has received from many members of his
congregation.

The High Calling follows Wingo's career through to maturity. His religion and his tolerance deepen, but his sturdy independence is not diminished. He has a rather fine denomina-
tional loyalty, though he is also greatly concerned with the
scandal of the disunity of the Churches. He has a moving defense of the Baptists, which none of our satirists can achieve. He
is defending a rather insignificant brother minister, and says
that you can often tell a Baptist simply by looking at him:

Brother Oliphant had that sort of tight look around his mouth. An
offensive-defensive look. It is pretty common among people who have
been pushed around. . . . Baptists are not persecuted in this country, but
we are ridiculed. It is partly our fault. We are aggressive one minute
and defensive the next. . . . We are the Plain People. A peculiar people.
Baptists of all people should understand the evils of anti-Semitism, for
in many ways we are like the Jews. . . . We scorn the ancient Jewish

idea of God's chosen people and contend we are Christ's chosen people.
. . . We practise spiritual exclusiveness and demand social inclusiveness.
. . . Like most of us Brother Oliphant is in a spiritual turmoil without
knowing why. He believes in a brotherhood through Christ, but on
Baptist terms.

. . . Our faith grew out of one of the most liberal and democratic
movements of all Christendom. We have abused it. I am often ashamed
of Baptist practices, but never of Baptist principles.[20]

This volume, *The High Calling*, has also an excellent discussion of the problems attendant upon a religious revival.
Wingo steers the middle course between utter skepticism as to
its value, and the equally dangerous method of forcing a spontaneous phenomenon to be prolonged by artificial pressures.
His remarks to a scoffing fellow minister are worth consideration: 'But we preachers are always talking about a spiritual
renaissance. Would we recognize one if we met it in the middle
of the road? We are waiting for it to come by edict or fiat. . .
It's not coming that way. It's got to begin with the hearts of
men.' Earlier in this same discussion he had replied to the suggestion that the revival in his church was a mere side-show, a
circus booth for the emotional performers: 'Harry—this is not
a side-show. And as for people laughing—well, let me tell you
something, brother, I have an idea some people laughed at the
ragged multitude that went up on the Mount. And I'll bet they
laughed at John the Baptist, standing waist-deep in Jordan and
baptizing sinners and preaching repentance.'[21]

If there is one warning that Street sounds repeatedly, it is
don't be beaten by a sneer or a snide remark! How Wingo deals
with the sarcasms of his friend, the radio station proprietor,
Benton, is heart-warming. Here is the kind of explosion we
should all wish to make on the right occasion! Benton has pooh-
poohed the revival as a hoop-de-do, and tells Wingo to close
down his show and return to his regular pitch. This is hardly
warranted from an agnostic! Wingo replies quietly but firmly:

'We will have no more of that, Benton. Not another word. You don't come into my house and talk that way. You or no other man.'

'You needn't get so upset . . . Maybe I was a little sarcastic.'

'Sarcastic!' London felt the flush higher on his face. 'Sarcasm is a weapon that only the very wise can use. Yours is not even honest sarcasm. It is smirking superiority, and I, for one, am sick of it.'

'Wait a minute,' Benton protested.

But the floodgate was down. . . . 'You've needled and needled, and I have had enough. Most agnostics I have known are intellectual zombies. Too proud to believe in God and too scared to deny Him . . . And your atheists are a bunch of narrow zealots who'd put any backwoods preacher in the shade. I've never ridiculed your smug little anthill, and don't you ridicule my mountain.'[22]

It was meant to clear the air—it only led to recrimination. It is not the least part of the meaning of James Street's novels that he brings before us the often undramatic but central themes and actions illustrative of Faith, Courage, Brotherhood, and Forgiveness, and his minister is a credible, unhaloed hero.

Divines in Doubt

IT HAS been customary in England, if not in America, to regard the nineteenth as the stolid century, in which the monarchy, the empire, the architecture, and the furniture are solid, safe, dependable, and unexciting. 'Respectable' is the epithet unhesitatingly applied to it and to the men who march resolutely across the Victorian stage, their sober faces made squarer by side-whiskers, and the prolific women who recline, as far as the horse-hair bristles and their bustles permit, on the sofas of the century. It was a stiff, rigid-backed, whale-boned, chins-up, aspidistra age. Such, at least, it seems from the vertiginous viewpoint of the present 'aspirin age.'

In fact, however, it was a period of revolution in politics, science, philosophy, art, and theology. *In Memoriam, Das Kapital* and *The Origin of Species* are all Victorian explosions in the world of thought. Even the quiet country parishes of the Church of England reverberated to the passionate pleas of the Evangelicals as they hammered at the sides of their pulpits, when they were not being summoned by the Tractarians as the Anglican Church Militant. In the realm of Biblical theology there were major earthquakes, as first the literal inerrancy of the Holy Scriptures was assailed by Higher Criticism, and then the very historicity of the Saviour of the Church was denied by the rationalists, and ultimately the cast-iron theology of

Divine decrees of Calvinism was fragmentated by the new liberalism and by Christian Socialism. 'Change and decay in all around I see,' seems to us a twentieth-century theme, but these are Victorian words to describe a Victorian experience. No period since the Reformation of the sixteenth century has caused so much heart-searching, so much doubt and anxiety, for honest men who wished to keep their religious faith abreast of contemporary culture. The very term 'agnostic' is a Victorian invention, attributable to Thomas Henry Huxley, who himself illustrates the perplexity of those who could neither affirm nor deny the existence of God. The three novelists selected present us with ministers as interpreters of religion in a period of cultural crisis, as anxious exponents of faith in a time of doubt and theological reconstruction.

1. William Hale White ('Mark Rutherford')

The Autobiography of Mark Rutherford, edited by His Friend Reuben Shapcott (1881)[1] and its sequel *Mark Rutherford's Deliverance* (1885) are, in effect, the spiritual diaries in novel form of William Hale White, who, in his agonizing doubts, believed himself to be a victim of his own century. The first novel shows us the process by which Mark Rutherford came to lose the simplicity and depth of his traditional Calvinistic faith: its sadness is the misery of negation in which the figure of the God-man, since the reading of Strauss's *Leben Jesu,* has dissolved into 'mythologic vapour.' The second novel records how, by strenuous thought and agonizing re-appraisal, he had come to arrive at some 'fortifying thoughts' by means of re-interpreting Christianity, with the aid of Wordsworth, Spinoza, and Hegel, as a religion of ideas and truths movingly exemplified in Jesus of Nazareth, but a religion, nonetheless, stripped of supernaturalism.

As Mark Rutherford looks at the rigid, Sabbatarian, predestinarian Calvinism of his youth, he is highly critical of its formalism and its unreality. He refers sardonically to the long, meandering prayers in which 'our minister seemed to consider that the Almighty, who had the universe to govern, had more leisure at His command than the idlest lounger at a club.'² He is equally critical of the long sermons which always repeated the same formulae: 'The minister invariably began with the fall of man, propounded the scheme of redemption, and ended by depicting in the morning the blessedness of the saints, and in the evening the doom of the lost.'³ But the unreality of this religion was revealed in its requirement that he should be 'converted' before being admitted to membership of the church, although he had no such experience. In the same kind of unreal trance, or spiritual sleep-walking, he was forced by his parents to decide on the ministry as a career, though his own preference had been for the life of an artist.

While still in the theological college Mark Rutherford was already beginning to sprout the horns of heresy, since he was convinced that theology had to be related to the *needs* of men. In this spirit he attempted to provide what might be called a 'functional' doctrine of the Atonement:

I began by saying that in this world there was no redemption for man but by blood; furthermore, the innocent had everywhere and in all time to suffer for the guilty. It had been objected that it was contrary to our notion of an all-loving Being that He should demand such a sacrifice; but, contrary or not, in this world it was true, quite apart from Jesus, that virtue was martyred every day, unknown and unconsoled, in order that the wicked might somehow be saved. This was part of the scheme of the world, and we might dislike it or not, we could not get rid of it. The consequences of my sin, moreover, are rendered less terrible by virtues not my own. I am literally saved from penalties because another pays the penalty for me. The atonement, and what it accomplishes for man, were therefore a sublime summing up as it were of what sublime

men have to do for their race; an exemplification, rather than a contra-
diction, of Nature herself, as we know her in our own experience.[4]

The president of the college said that this kind of teaching
might do in a cultivated congregation, but not for the country
church for which Rutherford was evidently intended. This
chill criticism introduced a deep self-distrust in Rutherford.

His first charge was the Water Lane Independent (the older
name for Congregational) Church in the eastern counties. It
had seen better days. Its deacons were small-town and small-
minded, conventional folk, including a farmer, an undertaker,
and the hand-rubbing subservient owner of a drapery store, Mr.
Snale. In the Dorcas needlework parties of the ladies, the minister was expected to engage that fragment of their attention
that was not concentrated on their fingers by readings from
suitable literature. Mr. Snale officiously ruled out *The Vicar of
Wakefield* as improper in mixed company, and George Fox's
Journal because the author was not a Congregationalist! Such
were the intellectuals before whom the aspiring theologian
cast his pearls. Even his attempts to provide special sermons
for special occasions, as at the Christmas season, were heard
unthanked. Becoming increasingly lonely and misunderstood,
he felt a closer affinity with the historic Jesus. He preached that
Jesus was a solitary thinker confronted by the enormous double
threat of the Jewish hierarchy and the Roman state, and in consequence, 'taught the doctrine of the kingdom of Heaven; He
trained Himself to have faith in the absolute monarchy of the
soul.' Rutherford went on to assert: 'Christianity was essentially
the religion of the unknown and of the lonely; of those who
are not a success.'[5]

Again the irony of the author shows itself when his chief
character, though a minister, can only find a kindred soul in
the atheist, Mardon, who joins him in a public meeting called

to protest against the town's cesspools which are a danger to the community's health. An anonymous letter, obviously the work of the sniveling Snale, printed in the town's newspaper, impertinently suggests that the minister should not interfere in politics and concludes with the sanctimonious information that Rutherford should only concern himself with the 'Water of Life' instead of suggesting policies that will add taxes to the overburdened poor. Mardon is as honest as Rutherford is, and, indeed, represents in the extreme form the most pressing criticisms which Hale White had to offer against the Christian faith.

Under the barrage of Mardon's criticisms, Rutherford begins a period of the most intense doubt. He finds himself even forced, in reply to the assertion of the contradictions in the Gospel records, to claim that if Jesus never lived yet the Christ-idea is a sublime and inspiring one. This argument Mardon rejects on the ground that if Jesus did not exist, how can the imitation of Christ be anything more than the merest hypothesis? That, he suggests, is a mere mirage. Mardon's talk darkened his nights and days. The novel reaches the abyss, with this cry of dereliction:

> With me the struggle to retain as much of my creed as I could was tremendous. The dissolution of Jesus into mythologic vapour was nothing less than the death of a friend dearer to me than any other friend I knew.[6]

His doubts have now become so persistent that there is hardly an article of the orthodox faith that he holds as true. He can only retain his preaching role by 'taking Scripture characters, amplifying them by hints in the Bible, and neglecting what was supernatural.'[7] This ruse worked only because of the isolation of the town and the ignorance of his congregation. Once again it is an anonymous letter that spells trouble for Mark Ruther-

ford, and the poison pen that wrote it was, of course, Snale.
Purporting to be a visitor to the town, Snale writes that he is
disturbed by the 'German gospel' which is preached from the
Water Lane pulpit. Hurt by this underhand attack, the minister
confronts Snale in his shop, and challenges him with the authorship which, for a while, he is too cowardly to affirm or to deny.
Snale, knowing that concealment is useless, then insinuates that
Rutherford is unreliable because he has broken an engagement
with his fiancée and because he is the friend of an atheist and his
daughter. Goaded beyond endurance, the minister cries out,
'Mr. Snale, you are a contemptible scoundrel and a liar.'[8] As
this subservient, oily man is the chief deacon, Rutherford knows
that his tenure of his office will shortly be terminated, so he re-
signs before he is expelled.

In his perplexity as where to seek his next employment as a
minister, he consults with Mardon. The latter insists that if he
is to preach elsewhere, as he proposes to do, a set of beliefs is
a necessity. At the same time Mardon denies that Rutherford
has any rationally defensible beliefs other than what he, Mardon, has. Challenged, Rutherford insists that he believes in God
and that He is the intellect of which the laws of the universe
are an expression. Mardon, however, claims that such an intellect is indifferent toward its own creation:

> It is an intellect, if it be an intellect at all, which will swallow up a city,
> and will create the music of Mozart for me when I am weary; an intel-
> lect which brings to birth His Majesty King George IV, and the love of
> an affectionate mother for her child; intellect which, in the person of a
> tender girl, shows an exquisite conscience, and in the person of one or
> two religious creatures whom I have known, shows a conscience almost
> inverted.[9]

Rutherford can only insist that he refuses to believe that this
is a mindless universe, and that an inner sentiment assures him

of this. Mardon pooh-poohs the very idea of sentiment and the discussion is over.

In fact, however, Rutherford now becomes a Unitarian minister to a congregation of seventeen souls, representing about five families. But these, too, are living on affirmations of the past; indeed, their convictions are chiefly negative, consisting largely of the denial of the orthodox doctrine of the Holy Trinity. The sheer formalism of Unitarianism is symbolized by a manuscript of a funeral sermon which had been left in the leaves of the pulpit Bible. This had praised in great detail the virtues of the deceased, but had done duty on several occasions, as was indicated by the changing of the masculine pronouns to feminine ones whenever appropriate. The dead hand of negation lay heavily upon Unitarianism; 'Although my congregation had a freethought lineage, I do not think that I ever had anything to do with a more petrified set . . . so far as I could make out the only topics they delighted in, were demonstrations of the unity of God from texts in the Bible, and polemics against tri-theism. Sympathy with the great problems then beginning to agitate men, they had none.'[10] There was only one exception, the simple but admirable Mrs. Lane. She was a great Bible reader who realized that the essence of faith was to be expressed not in the realm of the intellect, but in that of personal relationships. This generous woman was one in whom charity always prevailed; in the others it was always expediency. He found to his chagrin that the Unitarians had less capacity for personal affection than the Congregationalists. During this period he was merely 'playing the vagrant in literature, picking up here and there an idea which attracted me, and presenting it to my flock on the Sunday.'[11] Failing to excite others with these ideas, resignation was inevitable. His life was the bleaker as Mary Mardon had rejected his suit to devote the rest of her life to her ailing father. This is an especially sig-

nificant event for the author, for he always believed that the
two most tragic events in life were the loss of God and the loss
of love, which he always correlated. When Rutherford, in the
second novel, finds his 'Deliverance,' it is not only a new faith
but a new human friendship, too, in his marriage with Ellen
Butts. For Hale White believed that 'In the love of a woman
to the man who is of no account, God has provided us with a
true testimony of what is in His own heart.'[12] Rutherford was
now without faith and bereft of a response to his love.

Next he thought of becoming a schoolmaster, but his tenure
of his first post was only a day, so appalled was he by the insensibility of the headmaster and the indifference of his pupils.
He next became the assistant to a skeptical publisher and bookseller, Wollaston, who employed him only because he had
doubts about the Biblical miracles. Here he had some privacy
and comfort in Wollaston's menage, and his niece, also of a
vigorous intellectual frame of mind, showed great kindness to
Rutherford. In real life the publisher was Chapman of the firm
Chapman and Hall, and the 'niece' who befriended Hale White
was none other than Marian Evans, then the junior editor of
The Westminster Review and the future 'George Eliot.' So impressed was he by her practical sympathy that in her honor he
wished to make one addition to the Beatitudes: 'Blessed are
those who heal us of our self-despisings.'[13]

He met Mary Mardon in the bookseller's shop, where she
had gone to seek some skeptical literature for her father, who,
he learned, was mortally stricken. Visiting the dying Mardon,
he found that the atheist was able to confront death without
any fear, although he had no belief in a hereafter. He chilled
Rutherford's heart by arguing that there were two cogent
reasons against a belief in life after death. The first was: 'Is it
really desired by anybody that he should continue to exist for
ever with his present limitations and failings?' The second was

that 'a man ought to rid himself as much as possible of the miserable egotism which is so anxious about self' and its continuance beyond death.[14] The gray novel ends with an account of Mardon's death and his bleak funeral service, mirror of Mark Rutherford's bleak doubts and paralyzing uncertainties.

****

The hero is introduced in the sequel, *Mark Rutherford's Deliverance*, in a more hopeful situation, and, if the predominating color never reaches the radiance of gold, it has at least the silver of resignation. Three factors contribute to the 'Deliverance' of Rutherford: in his changed job, that of a parliamentary press correspondent to two papers, he finds an understanding friend in M'Kay, a man who, like himself, is profoundly religious while finding traditional formulations of theology unacceptable; later, he meets his former jilted fiancée, Ellen, now a widow, and ultimately marries her; and, most important of all, he and M'Kay arrive at a more satisfactory rationale for their faith and a practical way of serving humanity.

In this novel, Hale White's diatribes are reserved for the religiously or atheistically complacent, and for the impact of the Industrial Revolution on the great masses of the poor in the city of London. He and his new-found friend M'Kay tour the pulpits and platforms of the metropolis on Sunday mornings. After standing in line for a popular preacher, they are offended by the irrelevance of the first observation that he makes: 'My friends, I appeal to those of you who are parents. You know that if you say to a child "go," he goeth, and if you say, "come," he cometh. So the Lord. . .'[15] M'Kay, who had children and knew how disobedient they could be, nudged Rutherford and they left immediately. This is Hale White's way of emphasizing the triteness of orthodox ministers and the passivity of congregations even when they hear what flatly contradicts their own experience.

The rebels are not more satisfied with what they hear at free-thinking assemblies, which merely ridicule rather than reconstruct religious faith. One morning they attended a debate between a 'celebrated Christian' (who is believed to have been the famous Anglican Benedictine monk, Father Ignatius) who undertook to defend the Divine authority of the Old Testament, and his rationalist opponent. The 'celebrated Christian' seemed to imply that disbelief was merely sin, so he began with a fervent prayer for the conversion of his hearers and continued with the threadbare defense of the appeal to prophecy, and concluded with a rhetorical flourish referring to the Cross. His opponent merely resorted to the equally old chestnuts of the immorality of the patriarchs of Israel and the greed of the bishops of the Church of England. Rutherford's laconic conclusion is: 'To waste a Sunday morning in ridiculing such stories as that of Jonah was surely as imbecile as to waste it in proving their verbal veracity.' Clearly, some third alternative must be found to reconcile faith with intellectual honesty and practical compassion.

With M'Kay as the chief organizer the two friends determine to provide a small spiritual oasis in the desert of London slums. This took the form of a room they rented near Parker Street, Drury Lane. At the first meeting, at which perhaps thirty persons were present,

M'Kay announced his errand. The ignorance and misery of London were he said intolerable. . . . He proposed to keep this room open as a place to which those who wished might resort at different times, and find some quietude, instruction, and what fortifying thoughts he could collect to enable them to endure their almost unendurable sufferings. Anything which would be serviceable he would set forth, but in the main he intended to rely on holding up the examples of those who were

greater than ourselves and were our redeemers. He meant to teach
Christ in the proper sense of the word. Christ is now admired probably
more than He had ever been. Everybody agrees to admire him, but
where are the people who really do as He did? . . . He would try and
get them to see things with the eyes of Christ, to love with His love, to
judge with His judgment. . . . He trusted to be able, by means of this
little meeting, gradually to gain admittance for himself and his friends
into the houses of the poor and do some practical good.[16]

Hale White pours his own passionate indictment of the Industrial Revolution into the observations of Rutherford on the
slums of London and the desperate need for this little island of
quiet and compassion in Drury Lane:

It was an awful thought to me, ever present on those Sundays, and
haunting me at other times, that men, women, and children were living
in such brutish degradation, and that as they died others would take
their place. Our civilization seemed nothing but a thin film or crust lying
over a volcanic pit, and I often wondered whether some day the pit
would not break up through it and destroy us all. Great towns are
answerable for the creation and maintenance of the masses of dark, im-
penetrable, subterranean blackguardism, with which we become ac-
quainted. The filthy gloom of the sky, the dirt of the street, the absence
of fresh air, the herding of the poor into huge districts which cannot be
opened up by those who would do good, are tremendous agencies of
corruption which are active at such a rate that it is appalling to reflect
what our future will be if the accumulation of population be not
checked. To stand face to face with the insoluble is not pleasant.[17]

All the friends could do was to rescue a few despairing souls
from the maelstrom which would engulf them, such as a poor
coal porter, and a waiter who worked from nine in the morning
to almost an hour past midnight and whose wife was a desperate
drunkard.

The most important parts of the novel are those which suggest, rather than define, the reconstruction of religion in the
mind of Mark Rutherford. The salient features of the new re-

ligion seem to be two: intellectually an attempt is made to re-
shape the basic convictions of the older orthodoxy in a way to
meet modern need, and in this manner God becomes not the
miraculous breaker of the scientific laws but their guarantor;
morally, the imperatives of the New Testament still stand, with
Jesus as their great exemplar, and the incentive to all compassionate concern for the poor and the lonely.

Since Mark Rutherford proceeds much further in reconstruction than Mrs. Humphry Ward's hero, Robert Elsmere, his reformulations are of particular interest. Conversion he interprets
as the expulsive power of a new affection that redeems people;
'the exact counterpart of conversion, as it was understood by
the apostles, may be seen whenever a man is redeemed from vice
by attachment to some woman whom he worships, or when a
girl is reclaimed from idleness and vanity by becoming a
mother.'[18] Faith is life-committal to the idea of the supremacy
of the soul over all circumstances, 'the Kingdom of Heaven is
within you,' and Christ is man's Saviour only because He is an
unflinching martyr to the idea. Christ also witnesses to the supreme value of love and friendship for the unloved and un-
befriended. A man or woman who takes pity on others, who
have only their need to recommend them, becomes as it were
a little Christ in this compassion. But the two supreme doctrines
that Christianity teaches are the distinction between right and
wrong, and the duty of resignation and contentment. Of the
former Mark Rutherford remarked that to Philosophy, proclaiming the unity of our nature, every passion was as natural
as a saint-like action of negation, but that Christianity 'laid an
awful stress on the duality in us, and the stress laid on that
duality is the world's salvation. . . Its doctrine and its sacred
story are fixtures in concrete form of precious thoughts pur-
chased by blood and tears.'[19] The second major emphasis in
Christianity, according to Mark Rutherford, is in making it our

duty of duties 'to suppress revolt, and to submit calmly and come cheerfully to the Creator.'[20] In this reconstruction, there are evidences of the influence of Spinoza, Hegel, Carlyle, and Emerson; but the net result is far from the radiance and hope of historic Christianity. The resignation to God, which Hale White counsels, is a submission to the healing of Nature at times, and at other times, a heavy dose of Stoicism with a mild tincture of Christianity. He did, however, see Jesus as the hero of the moral life and the inspiration of the ages. It was something to have found this rock in the menacing seas of doubt, even if it was so much less than St. Paul had meant by Christ as The Rock.

2. *Mrs. Humphry Ward*

Robert Elsmere, which appeared in 1888, was the most widely read of all novels dealing with the problem of religious doubt in the Victorian age. It was a continuing topic of discussion in cultural circles and Gladstone's essay-review of it in the May 1888 issue of *The Nineteenth Century* is an indication of the alarm that it created in the minds of the orthodox, despite the Grand Old Man's sympathy with its honest intentions.

Robert Elsmere, then, is the narrative of the hero's duties as an Anglican vicar with a country parish in Surrey, of his growing doubts and reluctant resignation of his holy orders, of his reconstruction of faith and life, and of his foundation of a new Company of Jesus, 'The Order of Brotherhood,' in the London slums. Its rather inadequate inspiration is a Unitarian theology with a deep sense of compassion modeled upon the character of Jesus of Nazareth. In addition to its careful analysis of the decay of Elsmere's belief in orthodox Christianity, which will be reviewed in detail, it presents a gallery of varying attitudes to religion. Catherine Leyburn, Robert's wife, is an admirable study of strong and unyielding Evangelicalism. So strong is her Calvinistic sense of duty and 'calling' (like Ellen Butts), that it will not even allow her to contemplate marrying the man she loves until she is assured that this will not leave her widowed mother and two younger sisters disconsolate. It is typical that her favorite quotation from George Herbert reads: 'Thy Saviour sentenced joy.' When her husband, in her view, 'defects' to Unitarianism, she maintains her Evangelical loyalties for her child's sake and in the hope of her husband's eventual return to orthodoxy. The other type of orthodoxy portrayed, also with great vigor and sympathy, is the Tractarian High Churchman, Father Newcome, who has slaved for ten years in the slums of London, finding that the only way to quell doubt is to punish it with mortification and sacrifice. Langham and Grey, two Oxford tutors, represent two types of skepticism: the former is the symbol of the doubt that paralyzes and withdraws him from society and normal human relationships; the second, Grey, is the type that lives a happy family life and is strongly engaged in founding idealism on the ruins of Biblical criticism, and is especially fitted to be the mentor of Robert Elsmere, who also desires to accept Christian morality while discarding Christian mythology. There is a brilliant portrait of the aesthete in Rose Leyburn, and a remarkable sketch of a savant, Roger Wendover, whose historical researches have led him into atheism.

The chief value of the novel, however, is its careful documentation of the rise and fall of the Christian faith in Robert Elsmere and his attempt to reconstruct it. This, was, indeed, the great intellectual problem of the Victorian age to which Mrs. Humphry Ward addressed herself. She shows her hero turning to the ministry for inadequate reasons. He is exhausted by the life of an Oxford fellow and in his illness determines to seek a quiet country pastorate. This becomes available to him through the kindness of his great-uncle who, in his will, had

stipulated that Robert should be presented to the living of Murewell, should he ever take holy orders. At this period religion
means for him chiefly two things: the opportunity to incul-
cate and exemplify Christian morality and compassion, and the
aesthetic thrill of tradition. Oxford had woven her medieval
spell about his heart as an undergraduate in the university:

> As he sat in the undergraduate's gallery at St. Mary's on the Sundays,
> when the great High Church preacher of the moment occupied the
> pulpit, and looked down on the crowded building, full of grave, black-
> gowned figures, and framed in one continuous belt of closely-packed
> boyish faces; as he listened to the preacher's vibrating voice, rising and
> falling with the orator's instinct for musical effect; or as he stood up
> with the great surrounding body of undergraduates to send the melody
> of some Latin hymn rolling into the far recesses of the choir, the sight
> and experience touched his inmost feeling, and satisfied all the poetical
> and dramatic instincts of a passionate nature. The system behind the
> sight took stronger and stronger hold upon him; he began to wish
> ardently and continuously to become a part of it, to cast in his lot
> definitely with it.[21]

How could tradition not fail to thrill him where the ghosts of
Wycliffe, Cranmer, Wesley, and John Henry Newman walked
down the shadowy aisles?

As for his moral ardor, he was preparing to enter his parish
with the crusading zeal of the Christian Socialists, Maurice and
Kingsley. He read up 'the history, geology, and botany of the
Weald, and its neighbourhood, plunging into reports of agri-
cultural commissions, or spending his quick brain on village
sanitation.'[22] He made excellent use of this preparation and no
one was more formidable than he in challenging the Squire's
callous agent, Henslowe, or in demanding that the cottages of
Murewell be made more sanitary. In the tradition of 'muscular
Christianity' he encouraged the lads of the village to become
naturalists, whenever he could spare time from visiting the sick

or the perplexed souls of the community, by whom he was greatly beloved.

His basic trouble was that he had never thoroughly investigated the intellectual foundations of his faith. When he had told his tutor Langham he was considering the ministry, the latter had said sardonically, 'one may as well preach a respectable mythology as anything else.' Robert hotly asked for a definition of a mythology, to which his tutor answered, 'Simply ideas or experiences personified.' This Robert denied, asserting boldly, 'To the Christian, facts have been the medium by which ideas the world could not otherwise have come at have been communicated to man. Christian theology is a system of ideas, indeed, but of ideas realised, made manifest in facts.' Langham replied drily, 'How do you know they are facts?'[23] Elsmere's answer, being a compound of moral ardor and mysticism, showed only too clearly that it was not intellectual conviction that held him firmly to the traditional faith.

It is ironic that it is Elsmere's determination to reach Squire Wendover over the head of his callous factor, after the deaths of several villagers from diphtheria, that leads the vicar to know the atheist savant better and to be influenced by him more definitely.

Father Newcome tries to rescue Elsmere from the bog of historical criticism by warning him against the heresy of tolerance, which to the High Churchman's eyes was 'simply another name for betrayal, cowardice, desertion.' To this charge Elsmere replies, 'We are differently made, you and I . . . Where you see temptation, I see opportunity, I cannot conceive of God as the Arch-plotter against His own creation.'[24] Some months later Newcome's advice to Robert will be even more radical and frenzied. 'Trample on yourself! Pray down the demon, fast, scourge, kill the body that the soul may live! What are we, miserable worms, that we should defy the Most High, that we should set our feeble faculties against His Omnipotence?' Robert can only murmur in reply that 'All life is God's and all thought—not only a fraction of it.'[25]

Langham had seen that the entire case for orthodox Christianity rests on the credibility of the documents upon which it is based. To this investigation Robert Elsmere's association with the squire drives him. In his naturalist's studies he is being driven to the idea of evolution, and it is obvious that he must admit the validity of the same conception in historical studies also. Wendover, admiring the intelligence of Elsmere, wishes him ultimately to publish the squire's incomplete researches into the history of ideas. In a lengthy and decisive conversation with Elsmere he propounds his thesis that eras of history are only to be understood by reading and evaluating them in the light of the dominant ideas and intellectual preconceptions of the age. He then exemplifies his thesis from the early history of Christianity:

> In the first place, I shall find present in the age which saw the birth of Christianity, as in so many other ages, a universal preconception in favour of miracle—that is to say, of deviations from the common norm of experience, governing the work of *all* men of *all* schools.

He then goes on to urge that the testimony of the times must be read in the light of this, and with the result that

> the witness of the time is not true nor, in a strict sense, false. It is merely incompetent, half-trained, pre-scientific, but all through perfectly natural. The wonder would have been to have a life of Christ without miracles. The air teems with them. The East is full of Messiahs. The Resurrection is partly invented, partly imagined, partly ideally true—in any case wholly intelligible and natural, as a product of the age, when once you have the key of that age.[26]

This key, indeed, unlocks the history of ideas, but it also locks out Christianity from the serious consideration of the rational man. To this challenge Elsmere might formally reply that Christianity did not rest upon external historical evidence, but on the witness of faith in the human soul, but he knew that this was only whistling in the dark. The next three months of doubt were the bitterest days of his life.

He was now, indeed, in the hands of the Biblical critics and reconstructionists, and when light came in his darkness it would take the form of 'the image of a purely human Christ—a purely human, explicable, yet always wonderful Christianity. It broke his heart, but the spell of it was like some dream-country where-in we see all the familiar objects of life in new relations and perspectives.'[27] The change in his convictions was rendered doubly bitter because it divided him from the elder generation of Christians and even from his own wife. As Mrs. Humphry Ward says: 'And meanwhile half the tragedy of our time lies in this perpetual clashing of two estimates of life—the estimate which is the offspring of the modern spirit, and which is for-ever making the visible world fairer and more desirable in mortal eyes; and the estimate of St. Augustine.'[28]

One major consequence of his doubt is that not only must he cease to be vicar of the parish but he must also give up holy orders, and at a time when he had won the confidence of the entire parish, as had his wife Catherine. Others holding the Liberal Churchman's position might feel that they could con-tinue in the Church's ministry, undertaking its humane and charitable work while refusing assent to its dogmatic system; for himself 'it would be neither right nor wrong, but simply impossible.'[29] He comforted himself with Grey's favorite axiom that 'Conviction is the conscience of the mind.' Before making the final decision he goes up to Oxford to consult Grey, who offers him both sympathy and an encouragement in the lonely path he is treading. Grey understands how bereft he is without belief: 'I know very well, the man of the world scoffs, but to him who has once been a Christian of the old sort, the parting with the Christian mythology is the rending asunder of bones and marrow. It means parting with half the confidence, half the joy of life!' His last word is a reminder that the path of doubt is God's pedagogical method: 'It is the education of God! Do not imagine it will put you farther from Him! He is in criticism, in science, in doubt, so long as the doubt is a pure and honest doubt, as yours is.' God is to be sought in the soul of man, in the verifications of experience, and in the sacrificial giving of Christian love,' and 'All things change—creeds and philosophies and outward systems,—but God remains!'[30]

He and Catherine when they leave for life in London are too broken-hearted to take a farewell of the people at Murewell. Slowly but surely Elsmere takes up the broken fragments of his life again. He links himself with a group of Unitarians who are engaged in settlement work in the slums amongst the more intelligent type of artisan. There in Elgood Street he determines to fight negative rationalism and Comteism by stressing the positive effects the Jesus of history had for the improvement of human morality and social welfare. His solution is the same as Mark Rutherford's, except that he has greater confidence and organizing power, a private income, and contacts with the influential. In time Elsmere gathers a lively group of intelligent workmen about him, and with their cordial assent suggests, 'Suppose we throw all our energies into the practical building of a new house of faith, the gathering and organizing of a new Company of Jesus?'[31] Technically, this faith was Unitarianism, but it was far removed from the cold negations that characterized the superior rejections of Rutherford's Unitarian congregation. It strove to serve the compassionate Christ in the contemporary necessities of the poor. Flaxman, a critical aristocrat assistant of Elsmere's, comes to write to his friends of the new forms into which the new gospel of modernism is poured in Elgood Street.

Prayers of petition are eliminated, but the service opens with a magnificent prayer of adoration in which the soul is placed in the presence of the Eternal. Then follows a reading from the life of Christ in which devotion to his example and intelligent exposition are commingled. This is not a cloistered but an everyday religion, so that the choice of hymns and psalms is carefully restricted, and each one of them is also sung in the homes of the workmen. Elsmere's Sunday School teaching has removed the halo from Christ, but the narrative of his sufferings is all the more poignant for the children who listen. But the most impressive of all Elsmere's innovations is the transformation of the midday meal in the workman's cottage into a simple sacrament. Flaxman entered into a carpenter's home at noon:

Inside was a curious sight. The table was spread with the midday meal. Round the table stood four children, the eldest about fourteen, and the youngest six or seven. At one end of it stood the carpenter himself in his working apron, a brawny Saxon, bowed a little by his trade. Before him was a plate of bread, and his horny hands were resting on it . . .

Something in the attitudes of all concerned reminded me, kept me where I was, silent.

The father lifted his right hand.

'The Master said, *This do in remembrance of Me.*'

The children stooped for a moment in silence, then the youngest said slowly, in a little softened cockney voice that touched me extraordinarily,—

'*Jesus, we remember Thee always.*'

It was the appointed response.[32]

To bring the long story to its close, we recall that by overwork and lack of concern for his health, Elsmere develops a serious lung complaint and is sent away to Algiers to spend his few

remaining weeks of life. He leaves, with the most affectionate
farewells of his co-workers in the Brotherhood, having made
all the arrangements necessary for maintaining his work after
his death. Mrs. Humphry Ward would have us believe that although there was poignancy in the loss of the traditional faith,
yet the gain of a reconstituted faith was a great compensation;
for it was more honest and more relevant to the needs of the
nineteenth century.

All in all, Mrs. Humphry Ward produced a remarkable novel
on the problems of doubt in modern religion, but she was un-
duly sanguine of the results that the reconstruction of belief
on the lines she suggests is likely to produce. Hale White had
no easy solutions to offer, but that is probably because he had
plumbed the depths of despair. Moreover, in neither novel do
we go to the very abyss where Kierkegaard and Dostoevski
have been. On the other hand, even though they take us into
neither the darkness nor the dazzle, we should not be ungrate-
ful for the lesser candles of the two Victorian authors.

3. Harold Frederic

The Damnation of Theron Ware, or Illumination (1896)[33]
cannot be regarded as merely an American *Robert Elsmere*,
even though its theme is the conflict between the old faith and
the new knowledge. The first difference is that Theron Ware
does not succeed in making any theological reconstruction, for
his lapse was moral not theological. In the second place, the
author's intention is not to plead for the recognition among
Christians of a legitimate place for honest doubt and for the
necessity for a revised theology. On the contrary, he interprets
the moral lapses of Theron Ware as resulting from the ambition to cut a figure in the world of culture, to the neglect and

even contempt of his simple congregation and his faithful wife. Furthermore, Frederic's novel gives a much more sympathetic account of the older generation in religion than do those of Mrs. Humphry Ward and William Hale White. He would seem to suggest rather the danger than the exhilaration of adopting the new thought and the emancipated manners of modern times. Furthermore, he has an extremely sophisticated treatment of the role of the Catholic enclave in a predominantly Protestant America. All in all, his novel is less propagandist in outlook than those of Mrs. Humphry Ward or Hale White.

The book begins with a contrast between the meek elders of Methodism and the brash and ambitious Theron Ware who has preached before the Conference. The author is clearly a *laudator temporis acti:*

The sight of these venerable Fathers in Israel was good to the eyes, conjuring up, as it did, pictures of a time when a plain and homely people had been served by a fervent and devoted clergy—by preachers who lacked in learning and polish, no doubt, but who gave their lives without dream of earthly reward to poverty and to the danger and wearing toil of itinerant missions through the rude frontier settlements. These pictures had for their accessories log-huts, rough household implements, coarse clothes, and patched old saddles which told of weary years of journeying; to even the least sympathetic vision there shone upon them the glorified light of the Cross and the Crown.[34]

Ware, believing he has made a mark on the trustees of the fashionable city church in which the Conference is meeting, is deeply disappointed to be sent off to Octavius, a town of many Irish immigrants where Methodists are few and not influential.

The bucolic restrictions of the place placed a formidable yoke (if not, indeed, a millstone) about the neck of Theron Ware, as he learned at the first meeting of his trustees. The

Bible-centered cultural Philistinism of the church is admirably expressed in the opening speech of Brother Pierce:

We are a plain sort o' folks in these parts . . . We walk here . . . in a meek an' humble spirit, in the straight an' narrow way which leadeth unto life. We ain't gone traipsin' after strange gods, like some people that call themselves Methodists in other places. We stick by the Discipline an' the ways of our fathers in Israel. No new-fangled notions can go down here. Your wife'd better take them flowers out of her bunnit afore next Sunday.[35]

No sooner had Ware recovered from this sally, than the next attack was upon him: 'Another thing: We don't want no book-learnin' or dictionary words in our pulpit.' Brother Pierce insists that what is wanted is hell-fire preaching, dangling sinners over the pit, and terrifying his hearers by lurid descriptions of the death-beds of Voltaire and Tom Paine, because this is what fills the anxious seat and brings in souls hand-over-fist. Furthermore, there must be no talk about having a choir or an organ.

Soon after this, Ware has a fateful encounter with a group of Irish wagon-makers who are carrying one of their stricken comrades to his home to die, where he meets an aspect of the religious world entirely unfamiliar to him—Roman Catholicism. Here he is introduced to the intelligent and cultured priest, Father Forbes, who is obedient to the discipline of the Church, but in his way is quite a modernist. Here, also, he encounters the wealthy, independent, and 'emancipatedly modern' female in the person of the Titianesque Celia Madden, who is an aesthete in her dress, her abandon, and her piano-playing. These new-found friends are attracted by his engaging sincerity and his unaffected zeal to be introduced to the world of culture. Little do they realize that this will have the ultimate effect of disillusioning him with his denomination, his congregation, and his wife; far less that he will interpret Celia's friendly interest as tantamount to a declaration of love.[36]

At the priest's house he is introduced to a formidable scientist and scholar, Dr. Ledsmar, a former medical practitioner who has turned to the dissimilar hobbies of biological experiment and Assyriology. Ware is anxious to cultivate Ledsmar's friendship because the Methodist minister is hoping to write a new life of Abraham. Asking Ledsmar if the German monographs give any additional extra-Biblical information on Abraham's sayings or doings, Father Forbes interrupts to lead him gently into the territory of historical criticism: 'I fear you are taking our friend Abraham too literally . . . Modern research, you know, quite wipes him out of existence as an individual. The word "Abram" is merely an eponym—it means "exalted father." Practically all the names in the Genesis chronologies are what we call eponymous. Abram is not a person at all: he is a tribe, a sept, a clan.'[37] Ware is even more startled by Ledsmar's reference to the Christ-myth. Yet the curious fact is that he never undergoes a crisis of doubt like Mark Rutherford or Robert Elsmere.

It is not surprising that this introduction to the world of esoteric scholarship and uninhibited thinking has an intoxicating effect on Theron Ware, particularly as his education has not equipped him to answer the challenge. What is far more disturbing is that his vanity should make him think that Celia Madden and her group should consider him as an equal. She adds to his perplexity by telling him that her cult is the Greek theology of the strong and the beautiful, and he foolishly believes that this emancipated woman wishes to leap into the shackles of an affair with him.

Already his liberation of mind is turning to an emancipation from loyalties. He finds the very idea of pastoral visitation a chore, but determines to concentrate on the worldlier members of his flock who would rather not talk shop, and for these he naïvely prepares by diligent newspaper reading!

His last moorings to the old faith are cut when he receives from Dr. Ledsmar a parcel of intellectual dynamite, consisting of six books, two of which were written by the celebrated modernist, Ernest Renan. He was particularly fascinated by *The Recollections of My Youth;* so intrigued, in fact, that he simulated sickness in order to avoid the prayer-meeting and keep on with the reading. This, too, is a sign of the disintegration of the man who once was honest. Yet while reading, Ware seems utterly unconscious of the fact that he is falling into the pit of a double intellectual standard—one for the humble believer and another for the rational, cultured man. Frederic comments, in a most perceptive analysis of the attractions of historical criticism and comparative religion:

Somehow, the fact that the priest and the doctor were not religious men, and that this book which had so impressed and stirred him was nothing more than Renan's recital of how, he too, ceased to be a religious man, did not take a form which Theron could look square in the face. It wore the shape, instead, of a vague premise that there were a great many different kinds of religions,—the past and dead races had multiplied these in their time literally into thousands,—and that each no doubt had its central support of truth somewhere for the good men who were in it, and that to call one of these divine and condemn all the others was a part fit only for untutored bigots. Renan had formally repudiated Catholicism, yet could write in his old age with the deepest filial affection of the Mother Church he had quitted. Father Forbes could talk coolly about the 'Christ-myth' without even ceasing to be a priest, and apparently a very active and devoted priest. Evidently there was an intellectual world, a world of culture and grace, of lofty thoughts and the inspiring communion of real knowledge, where creeds were not of importance, and where men asked of each other, not 'Is your soul saved?' but 'Is your mind well furnished?' Theron had the sensation of having been invited to become a citizen of the world. The thought so dazzled him that his impulses were dragging him forward to take the new oath of allegiance before he had had time to reflect upon what it was he was abandoning.[38]

Among the delights of this novel are the set-pieces that Frederic
introduces: the Methodist Conference, a Revivalist and Debt-
cancelling Meeting, and a Camp-Meeting in the woods, which
are remarkable for their accuracy and insight. In their way
they are as reliable an account of social history and of disappear-
ing practices in the older Methodism as Hale White's account
of the nineteenth-century chapel versus church ethos of the
ultra-sensitive Dissenters of the English midland counties.*
The hilarious account of how the debt-cancellers, Brother and
Sister Soulsby, turn a revival meeting into a fund-raising cam-
paign by playing off one trustee against another, after taking
the precaution of locking the church doors, is also a means of
introducing two shrewd but quite unpretentious Methodist lay
people into the book. The Soulsbys prove in the end for all their
lack of polish and culture to be the best friends of Ware and
his wife when the bottom falls out of their world.

Ware's vanity leads him into one gaucherie after another. He
tries to impress Celia that he is emancipated and, in fact, shocks
her by saying that he has been reading a novel by George Sand.
He makes a further *faux pas* when he tries to get Ledsmar to
tell him if there is anything sinister in the association between
Celia and Father Forbes.

His inner deterioration can be diagnosed from other signs. His
preaching degenerates into mere flamboyant rhetoric, while
his thoughts grow increasingly skeptical. He dallies with many
aspects of the case against revealed religion 'from the mild heterodoxy of Andover's qualms to the rude Ingersoll's rollicking negation of God Himself,'[39] considering himself free to postpone
indefinitely the duty of selection. He lost all sense of right and
wrong, and even bought a small book on the art of manicure!

---

* This gospel of culture is admirably satirized in a recent novel by another
American author, Peter De Vries, in *The Mackerel Plaza* to which reference
is made in Chapter VI.

When he has been a great success at a Methodist Camp-
Meeting in the woods, he finds relief in wandering away from
the site and there meets his Catholic friends at a church outing
with free beer. Here he expresses his complete disloyalty to his
faith, his congregation, and his wife. Father Forbes argues that
the Catholic Church will survive the present disbelief, but
Ware insists that 'the march of science must very soon produce a universal scepticism.'[40] Ware then propounds the outrageous sentiment that marriage is an encumbrance and a stony
silence ensues. His misery is completed a few moments later
when Celia's drunken brother blurts out an insinuation that
Ware has an indecent concern for his sister.

Despite this warning, and the far more serious warning of
another brother who is too near death to be concerned with
anything less than speaking the simple truth, the infatuated
Ware, learning that Celia and Father Forbes are going to New
York, steals the church money in a mad attempt to follow and
surprise her in her hotel room and ask her why she had refused
to see him. He in turn is shattered by the ugly truths that his
insensibility forces her to tell him. Her evaluation of Ware's
character is the novelist's own:

We liked you, as I have said, because you were unsophisticated and
delightfully fresh and natural. Somehow we took it for granted that you
would stay so . . . Instead we found you inflating yourself with all sorts
of egotisms and vanities. We found you presuming upon the friendships
which had been mistakenly extended to you . . . Your whole mind became an unpleasant thing to contemplate. You thought it would amuse
and impress us to hear you ridiculing and reviling the people of your
church, whose money supports you, and making a mock of the things
they believe in. You talked to us slightingly about your wife. What
were you thinking of, not to comprehend that you would disgust us? . . .
What you took to be improvement was degeneration. When you thought
you were impressing us most by your smart sayings and doings, you
were reminding us most of the fable of the donkey trying to play the
lap-dog. And it wasn't even an honest, straightforward donkey at that![41]

The final scene is that of a disgusting, rum-soaked, stubble-faced Ware begging for admission in the small hours to the Soulsby house and making his desperate confession to Mrs. Soulsby. He had tried to commit suicide after his pride has been exploded by Celia's condemnation, but this, like his attempt for three days to get drunk, had failed miserably. Ware and his wife Alice stay on in the home of the genuine Soulsbys for several months and it is they who procure him a post in Seattle as the superintendent of a real estate company. The Soulsbys had rightly decided that he was a misfit in the ministry. Our last glimpse of the incorrigibly vain and ambitious Ware is when he is already, in imagination, swaying great crowds with his political rhetoric and visualizing himself as the popular Senator for the state of Washington!

This novel, then, is not so much a study of the agonizing problem of correlating traditional faith with the new scientific and historical knowledge; it is chiefly a study of the disintegration of a minister through succumbing to vanity, in the form of intellectual ambition. If *Robert Elsmere* and the *Mark Rutherford* novels are admirable case studies of honest doubt and its dilemmas, *The Damnation of Theron Ware* is a perceptive analysis of dishonest doubt. Both experiences may befall the minister who tries to be the interpreter of faith in a time of cultural crisis, and the warnings in these novels have not ceased to be relevant in our own time.

IV

The Confessional
and the Altar

ALTHOUGH Catholic priests minister to a minority, albeit a large one, in the predominantly Protestant countries of the English-speaking lands, there are several reasons for considering the sympathetic place that the priest has in modern fiction. His calling is an ancient and an honorable one. It is, moreover, the type of Christian ministry that was and is most widely practiced in ancient and modern times in the entire world. Its asceticism has never failed to fascinate an indulgent world. Its certainties of dogma have worried the liberal and skeptical mind, but have been gratefully accepted by those who, like Chesterton, believed that there is only one thing for an open mind, as for an open mouth, to do, that is, to close it on something solid. The drama of the liturgy of which the priest is the celebrant speaks to the aesthetic sense of the man who is deaf to its divine doctrine. At a more superficial level, the distinctive garb of the priest or the monk or the friar, his *potestas*, his dedication to meditation, and his austerities, attract the playwright, the writer of film scenarios, and the novelist, much more than the Protestant minister, because of dramatic and aesthetic possibilities.

Whether we are Protestant, Catholic, or uncommitted, we shall be likelier to understand the role of the Roman Catholic priest the better by the imaginative interpretations of his calling offered by such Catholic novelists as Georges Bernanos, François Mauriac, and Graham Greene.

The basic differences between the Catholic priesthood and the Protestant ministry are, it seems, threefold. First, the priest's chief distinction is that he is the celebrant of the Eucharist, through which—and also in the other six sacraments—he is enabled to convey the grace of God. No matter whether he is a devoted priest, or a mediocre one; no matter whether he is handsome and eloquent or ugly and stuttering; no matter whether he is learned or simple his privilege is to perform, at Christ's institution, the miracle by which consecrated bread and wine become the very body and blood of Christ, God in the flesh, which is the medicine of immortality. Let him but place that on the tongue of a man who is not in mortal sin, and that man attains to immortality. The priesthood is indispensable and the sacraments are indispensable for the Catholics. You may take them or reject them; but no persuasion or wheedling is necessary on the part of the priesthood. The grace of God is objectified. By contrast the Protestant minister deals with the intangibles of faith; he has to persuade men to receive the Word of God and he must use his personality as the medium through which the Word comes relevantly to men.

In the second place, the priest is the confessor of souls and their director, and he is empowered to offer absolution. His authority, as being in the apostolic succession, as the representative of a really international and vast church with all the prestige of the centuries, and above all the authority that asceticism gives him, and his seminary training in casuistry, prepare him to be the anonymous recipient of the terrible secrets of the hearts of men. The dark confessional box in which he is hidden is the expected place for unburdening the soul. In Protestantism, a man is expected to confess his sins to God alone. Sometimes he does; more often he joins in a conventional confession in public. Almost never does he expect to make reparation for his sins. And it is rare for him to come to his pastor with the darkest burdens of sin.

In the third place, the priest is the director of the local branch of a vast church which undertakes all kinds of social responsibility for the variety of races and classes in his parish—and this gives him a standing in his own community that no Protestant minister is likely to possess in his. It also means that his asceticism, the political power of his church, and his prestige subject him to temptations which the Protestant minister does not feel to the same degree.

In the consideration of Catholic priests in fiction, it might be desirable for Protestants to be constantly asking three questions: (1) How can Protestant preaching be applied more directly to individual souls? (2) Does Protestantism sufficiently stress the objective facts and acts of God and make enough of the centrality of the Sacrament of Holy Communion? (3) Why are Protestant ministers not content more readily to be fools for Christ's sake, and to despise conformity?

G. K. Chesterton has suggested that every age turns for help to the saint that contradicts it most. He instances the attraction of the prosperous Victorian industrialists for St. Francis of Assisi—who was named the poor little man (*Il Poverello*) and who married Poverty as his bride—and suggests that the sheer relativities in morals and thought in our time have driven many intellectuals to the massive and co-ordinated system of Revelation and Reason built up by St. Thomas Aquinas in his *Summa Theologiae*. This attraction of opposites may help in part to explain the popularity of the priest in modern fiction. What is even more interesting is the attraction of the figure of a poor, simple, holy man in the priesthood.* Guareschi is writing about him in the *Don Camillo* series of novels, in which the simplicity of the priest outmaneuvers the shrewdness of the Communists. Chesterton's Father Brown (in his series of detective novels) is another variation on the same theme, except that his is the simplicity of integrity not of intelligence. But in our time the supreme fictional account of the fool for Christ's sake is undoubtedly found in Georges Bernanos' *The Diary of a Country Priest.* The two other fictional priests we have to consider are rather different in some respects. François Mauriac's Abbé Calou in *The Woman of the Pharisees* has an intelligence far surpassing that of the other country priest, but he is content to bear the criticism and obloquy of the world for Christ's sake. On the other hand, Graham Greene's whisky priest in *The Power and the Glory* is undisciplined, weak, shifty, a seducer, and morally an outcast, but even this earthiest of vessels is in his death a witness to the supernatural God in a Mexico which has proscribed all priests and all religion. Perhaps this is the most remarkable portrayal of all of the paradox of grace, that only the man who is utterly unaware of any virtue in himself may become a saint. It is also the most brilliant realization of the Catholic emphasis on the objectivity of the sacraments and of grace. Grace is mediated to men who are utterly unworthy through a representative who seems even more unworthy than those to whom he ministers, and is thereby more clearly the gift of God and not of the priest. It is also a remarkable testimony to the doctrine of justification by faith.[1]

---

* It is interesting to note that the characterization of the servant of God as a fool for Christ's sake is not peculiarly a Catholic interpretation, for Goldsmith used the conception in *The Vicar of Wakefield* for his Dr. Primrose, as did Fielding in his *Joseph Andrews* for Parson Adams. Eastern Orthodoxy, too, has its conception of the fool for Christ's sake in the characters of Father Zossima and Aloysha in Dostoyevski's *The Brothers Karamazov.*

1. Georges Bernanos

Bernanos wrote *Le Journal d'un curé de campagne* in 1936, and the English translation, *The Diary of a Country Priest*, which appeared the following year, was an instantaneous success. It was a document of conviction in an era of totalitarian appeasement. It was also the work of a writer who was profoundly concerned with social justice at a time when the stand of the Roman Catholic Church in Spain implied that Catholics were more interested in the perpetuation of social injustice. Bernanos was intending, it seems, to write the life of a modern Curé d'Ars, a man of extraordinary innocence, like a child and like the poor, yet the better a vessel for the reception of divine grace because his hands were utterly empty of pride. The historic curé, it might be mentioned, was reported to his superiors in the church for a multitude of sins, and when he was permitted to see this list of his offences, to make the document accurate he added two more, signed it, and sent it to his bishop. Such was the type of man Bernanos wished to present in his country priest, as a condemnation of the compromises so many priests and Christian laymen make with the world. Intended by his mother for the priesthood, Bernanos decided that he would be a Christian writer and apologist of the Catholic Church for those folk the usual priests would never be able to contact.

On the first page Bernanos tells us that the curé is bored with his parish because it has so few creative possibilities. This is to show us that there are no natural advantages in this parish and that it will be by grace alone that God will make his drudgery divine. This novel, written in the form of a diary, will inevitably consist very largely of meditations, not of action or the development of character. Hence the citations will chiefly be of the reflections, often not only apposite but moving and profound, that Bernanos makes on the role of the priesthood in the modern world.

A frequently reiterated point is that *ennui* is the enemy of hope and thus of salvation. To avoid it everyone is 'on the go' all the time, lest they should confront the awful despair, the ashes of life. Even the superior clergy were no longer official optimists; they teach optimism by force of habit, not from any conviction.

Time was when according to secular tradition a bishop's sermon had always to end with a prudent hint . . . of coming persecution and the blood of the martyrs. Nowadays these prophesies are becoming far more rare, probably because their realization seems less uncertain. [2]

One may note at this time that Graham Greene has this apocalyptic sense of coming doom, which Mauriac says is one of his finest characteristics as a Catholic novelist and realist.

The curé de Torcy, the friend of our country priest, has striking thoughts, though they are often too clever by half. Nowadays, the curé informs our priest, the great virtue is prudence, but the daring of faith and hope are denied by the preference for a commonsense calculation of risks. The priest has decided against prudence.

A worldling can think out the pros and cons and sum up his chances. No doubt. But what are *our* chances worth? We who have admitted once and for all into each moment of our lives the terrifying presence of God. . . What is the use of working out chances? There are no chances against God. [3]

Bernanos protests against the idea that Christians are milksops, careful, conventional, and timid.

A Christian people doesn't mean a lot of goody-goodies. The Church has plenty of stamina and isn't afraid of sin. On the contrary, she can look it in the face calmly and take it upon herself, assume it at times as our Lord did. When a good workman's been at it all the week, surely he is due for a booze on a Saturday night? Look: I'll define you a Christian people by the opposite. The opposite of a Christian people is a people grown old and sad.[4]

Peculiarly apt is the warning that a priest must expect cruel hardship and if he is faithful in the discharge of his duty must not expect to be popular. Yet what temptations there are both to be comfortable and to be popular, and therefore to be conformist! The curé de Torcy in warning his younger colleague, also warns others in the following exhortation:

The whining priests want bread with jam on it. Well, a man can't live on jam, neither can a Christian society. Our Heavenly Father said mankind was the salt of the earth, son, not the honey. And our poor world's rather like old man Job, stretched out in all his filth, covered with ulcers and sores. Salt stings on an open wound, but saves you from gangrene!

The priest of Torcy advises his young colleague against the folly of desiring to be loved. Too strongly, he insists that it is the duty of the priest to be respected and obeyed. But he gives a remarkable insight into the perennial task of the Catholic Church as he sees it:

What the Church needs is discipline. You've got to set things straight all the day long. You've got to restore order knowing that disorder will get the upper hand the very next day, because such is the order of things, unluckily: night is bound to turn the day's work upside down—night belongs to the Devil.[5]

But this is contrary to the Christian hope and to the fact of transformation of character through redemption. That is why the country priest does not wish to be moulded by this part of the advice.

If the country priest wishes for any quick success, he is certainly soon disillusioned. He soon understands that there is a

real danger in hoping for any attachment to the priest as a person, for apart from this being evanescent in character, it is also
a failure to attach souls to Christ. He learns this when he has
completed a catechism lesson and given the weekly prize to
Seraphita Dumouchel, a pert lass who seems to him to be sincerely zealous in her piety. He asks her:

'Aren't you longing to welcome Our Lord Jesus? Doesn't it seem a long
time to wait for your first Communion?'
'No,' she answered, 'why should it? It will come soon enough.' I was
non-plussed, but not greatly shocked, for I knew the malice there is in
children. So I went on:
'But you understand me, though. You listen so well.' Her small face
hardened and she stared.
'It's 'cause you've got such lovely eyes.'
Naturally I didn't move a muscle, and we came out of the sacristy together. All the other children were outside whispering and they suddenly stopped and shouted with laughter. Obviously, they'd planned
the joke together.'[6]

Is not the frequent attachment of a congregation to the ministry
instead of to Christ and His community a fearful failure on the
part of Protestant ministers, also?

The theme of the need for forthright preaching and speaking on the part of the priesthood is never far from Bernanos'
pen. He puts these strong words in the mouth of the priest from
Torcy, who is an enemy of those easy speeches and pleasant
phrases that comfort cruel men:

The Word of God is a red-hot iron. And you who preach it 'ud go
picking it up with a pair of tongs, for fear of burning yourself, you
daren't get hold of it with two hands. It's too funny! Why, the priest
who descends from the pulpit of Truth, with a mouth like a hen's vent,
a little hot but pleased with himself, he's not been preaching: at best he's
been purring like a tabby-cat. . .[7] And mind you many a fellow who
waves his arms and sweats like a furniture remover isn't necessarily
more awakened than the rest. On the contrary, I simply mean that when

the Lord has drawn from me some word for the good of souls, I know, because of the pain of it.[8]

The country priest is most careful with his visiting, and he offers a caution to over-programed churches and over-busy ministers of them.

I have undertaken to visit each family once every three months at least. My colleagues consider this excessive, and indeed such a promise will be hard to keep, since first and foremost I must not neglect a single duty. . . . There remains the unforeseen.

Note the latter words particularly. It would have been so much easier to satisfy a geometrical and moralistic God than the God who sends the unexpected, as Bernanos says later. But notice the importance of personal relationships, privately or in the family: these take precedence over programs and there is no thought at all about promotion! He even founds a sports club for youth, a little impractically since an industrial firm sponsors one in a neighboring parish, yet it is worth it for his contact with the few. He very readily accepts the injunction of the practical mystic Ruysbroeck who said:

Though you be caught up in the very rapture of God, and there come a sick man to demand of you a bowl of broth, descend again from your seventh heaven and give him that which he comes to ask.[9]

There is no attempt to save men here by the barrel-load, like a lot of herrings. There are no statistics, only infinitely valuable souls who must be threaded about the neck of the Church one by one, like pearls.

The profoundest lesson that the priest learns is that the deepest fellowship with Christ is in shared suffering.

More and more firmly [writes the country priest] am I convinced that what we call sadness, anguish, despair, as though to persuade ourselves

that these are only states of the Spirit, are the Spirit itself. I believe that
ever since his Fall, man's condition is such that neither around nor
within him can he perceive anything, except in the form of agony.[10]

He visits the doctor to learn that he has cancer in the stomach;
it bewilders him a little but he offers this also to God, as he says:

Dear God, I give you all willingly. But I don't know how to give, I just
let them take. The best is to remain quiet. Because though I may not
know how to give, You know how to take . . . Yet I would have wished
to be, once, just once, magnificently generous to You![11]

Far from being spectacular his death was even indecorous.
He dies in the attic room of a friend who is an unfrocked priest,
and no colleague can come in time to give him extreme unction.
So the curé, in his friend's soiled love-nest, asks the ex-priest for
absolution.

He gave it doubtfully. The curé was then told of his friend's regret that
the delay of a priest in coming threatened to deprive his comrade of
the final consolation of the Church. His final words were: 'Does it
matter? Grace is everywhere.'[12]

He died, as he lived, an unself-conscious and unpretending witness of grace, Christ's fool, but with the folly that is wiser than
the wisdom of men, and another witness to justification by
grace.

The most dramatic section of the book covers some thirty
pages and so by reason of its length is unquotable. It is the account of the curé's struggle for the proud soul of the countess,
who is encrusted with dignity, pride, and vindictiveness, and
thoroughly despises the curé for his peasant origin, poor clothes,
youth, and lack of savoir-faire. It is a magnificent and moving
portrayal of the interior drama of salvation where the humility
and truth of God's priest face and win a loving victory over
the pride and selfish illusions of a Pharisee. He bears all her in-

sults, her attempts to trap him into unguarded statements by diabolical subtlety; he parries with the penetration of God's poniard of truth that strips the veils of illusion away from her. Her bitterness springs from the death of her son, and the fact that her daughter is her father's favorite, while her husband himself is unfaithful. Only the finale of the dramatic encounter can be cited. He tells her that she must resign herself to God's will. This she pretends to do, but this is hypocrisy, as he sees when she says, with bitterness,

'I might have given up going to church altogether. But I considered that sort of thing beneath me.'
'Madame, no blasphemy you could utter would be as bad as what you've just said. Your words have all the callousness of Hell in them. How dare you treat God in such a way? You close your heart against Him.'

Then the priest realizes that at least the countess is no longer indifferent to God's existence. She breaks in again with excuses:

'At least I've lived in peace—and I might have died in it.'
'That's no longer possible.'

She protests:

'I've ceased to bother about God. When you've forced me to admit that I hate Him, will you be better off, you idiot?'

The priest:

'You no longer hate Him. Hate is indifference and contempt. Now at last you are face to face with Him.'

The transformation within the countess now takes an outward symbol. She removes her mantilla and takes from her neck a medallion on a plain silver chain, presses the cover with her finger nail, the glass falls out, and a little lock of golden hair twines about her finger. She is going to try to bargain with the priest that if she is converted, then she may share eternity with her dead child.

'Will you swear to me—' she began.
'My daughter,' he said (the word came to him spontaneously), 'God is not to be bargained with. We must give ourselves to Him unconditionally.'

She insists that he repeat again that Hell is to be always without love. He demands that she give everything to God. Immediately she throws the medallion straight into the glowing logs! The priest's sympathy forces him to try to retrieve the precious memento, but in vain, despite his burns.

'What madness,' he cries, 'How could you dare?'

She had retreated to the wall, which she leaned against.

'I'm sorry.' Her voice was humble.
'Do you take God for an executioner? Gods wants us to be merciful with ourselves. And besides, our sorrows are not our own. He takes them on Himself, into His heart.'
'My daughter,' said the priest, 'you must be at peace.'

He then blessed her and agreed to hear her confession the next day. He enjoined absolute silence and he promised absolute silence. He received from her the next day a letter saying that for eleven years after the loss of her child she had lost hope and now had regained it from the priest, who was like a child in his simplicity.

The curé's own part in this dramatic encounter is thus evaluated by him.

Our Lord had need of a witness, and I was chosen, doubtless for lack of any better, as one calls in a passer-by. I should be crazy indeed to imagine that I had a part, a real part in it. Already it is too much that God should have given me the grace to be present when a soul became reconciled to hope again—those solemn nuptials![13]

There is time not to detail, but only to mention the brilliant way that Bernanos evokes the original passion of Christ in the life of his country priest, so that the imitation of Christ is always being suggested.

For Bernanos, says Hans Urs von Balthasar in *Le Chrétien Bernanos,*

The saints are not only nor always men who come from God and who in their rapid flight towards Him, as it were open a breach in the Heavens, through which several rays of eternity fall down; they are primarily messengers who accompany Christ in His descent from God to the world, bearers of a word which may be silent, which may be said by their life, by their suffering, by their death, but is nonetheless a message addressed to men. They are themselves words, infinitely stronger and more profound than the poor words that men use, and all generations have as their consequent task the interpretation of these words.[14]

There is only one question which Bernanos poses indirectly to Protestants: Is it true that at the Reformation and afterwards Protestants dropped the honors degree of sainthood and raised the passing level? In other words, do they believe in sainthood as a retreading of the *via dolorosa?* If so, who are their candidates for canonization?

2. *François Mauriac*

In M. Mauriac we have to do with a novelist who has gained the highest recognition that his own civilized country can offer, membership in the Académie Française, and in the most anti-clerical and anti-Catholic era since the French Revolution.* Of his many admirable works, it is proposed to select only one, and that is known in the original as *La Pharisienne,* and is most

---

* Mauriac is also a Nobel Prize winner.

clumsily translated as *A Woman of the Pharisees*,[15] for it carries
no echo of the worldliness that *Parisienne*, so close a word to
Pharisienne in both sound and appearance, suggests.

This novel is selected because of the brilliant portrayal of the
lost innocence of youth (of which the Graham Greene script
of the film *Fallen Idol* is the English Catholic parallel), because
the Abbé Calou is Mauriac's fullest portrayal of a priest, and
because I do not know a subtler analysis in literature of a female Pharisee—an analysis so profound that he almost makes
us feel sympathy for this odious being who is also a soul, and
salvable. As Nelly Cormeau, Mauriac's official interpreter says:

The abbé Calou is opposed to the Woman of the Pharisees, like modesty
to ostentation, as humility to pride, as love to vindictiveness, as existence
to illusion. He is the Priest in essence, the incorruptible intercessor of a
religion all simplicity, disinterestedness and love.[16]

The stupendous image of the priest he draws in this novel is,
in his own unforgettable definition, of one 'who walks before
Grace as the dog precedes the invisible Hunter.'[17] His task is
merely to obey the commands of his invisible Master, to draw
the erring soul out of the thickets and tangles of illusion that it
may be stricken by the love of God. Mauriac believes that Christ
has to wage an unceasing war against His competitors for the
souls of mankind, and these are love in the sphere of human
relationship and Mammon in terms of material possessions.

The theme of this novel is the unfolding of the subtle self-de-
ception in the life of Brigitte Pian, the second wife of a weak
husband, a woman abounding in good works by which she
hopes to merit salvation, and yet who dominates the recipients
of her charities and saps them of their self-respect. She too
readily identifies her own will with the Divine will and wreaks
havoc in the lives of others, particularly in the case of M. Puy-
baraud (the schoolmaster and intended ascetic and cleric) and

the simple Christian woman he marries, who dies in childbirth. She makes them almost ashamed to marry by her insinuation that this is an unworthy decline from asceticism and humiliates them into utter subjection because of her control of employment opportunities. Her influence, in attempting to destroy the love of her ward and stepdaughter Michele for the wild and independent young aristocrat Jean de Mirbel, would—but for the intervention of Abbé Calou—have been successful. In the end Grace wins in its patient, subtle, and supernatural charitable struggle with sin and evil in her soul, and the minister of Grace to her, also, despite the fact that she has tried to silence and deprive him of his office, is the excellent Abbé Calou. Calou is a former theological professor whose Pascalian profundities and penetration caused him to be viewed with suspicion by his conventional superiors, and ultimately to be exiled to a remote country parish. He makes a speciality of trying to win wild, gifted, and wilful boys for God.

If hypocrisy—its origin in self-love and its cure in Christocentric self-abasement—is the dominant theme of this novel, the subordinate theme is the disillusionment of youth caused by the infidelity of a trusted adult relative. The most dramatic moment in the novel is when the adolescent Jean de Mirbel, having escaped from the presbytery of the abbé in his search for emotional security and desiring to surprise his mother at a country hotel, discovers that she, though a widow, has as a lover a middle-aged actor, a roué. He is heartbroken and can—in his misery—only climb onto a pile of hay. It is from this damp haystack, that he, racked with pleurisy, is rescued by the abbé. The abbé is the symbol of the Christ he serves. Though despised and rejected of men and women, though reported to the Cardinal, and though he loses even his small and insignificant curacy, he is ever forgiving, humble, unwearying in his cure of souls. Yet in his weakness and meekness there is a terrible strength—

the strength of Truth. It is with this *épée* that he probes motives and slashes illusions; he is unobtrusive, and yet the controlling character of the book. The greatest of Mauriac's many profiles of priests, yet never a plaster saint: a man with big hands, poor, unrecognized except by the few and often for the wrong reasons, the prey of the anti-clericalism of the chemist's poisonous wife, and often indiscreet and interfering in his spontaneity —these are spots on the sun, providing proof that God can make the ordinary man extraordinary by grace, yet always human and never improbable.

Among many admirable qualities worthy of imitation, one that must be emphasized is his unwillingness to be shocked by anything. He has fought with evil too long to be surprised by any of its stratagems or disgusted by its effects. He always loves the sinner, while understanding and yet abhorring his sins. One example will suffice. He will not gate-crash his way into the confidence of the boy. He has invited Jean de Mirbel, his charge, to enter the church, but the boy regards the church, and religion as a symbol of the servitude his callous military uncle has imposed upon him in putting him under M. Calou's charge. So he replies that he is not interested in such old-wives' tales. The rest follows in Mauriac's words:

'Really? That's interesting.' There was no other hint of outrage in M. Calou's tone.
'Does it surprise you?'
'Why should it?' said the curé. 'The really surprising thing is that a man *should* believe . . . The really surprising thing is that what we believe should be true. The really surprising thing is that the truth should really exist, that it should have taken on flesh, that I can keep it a prisoner here beneath these old vaults that don't interest you . . . Yes, you little oddity, I can never get over the feeling how absurd, how utterly mad, it is that what we believe should be precisely and utterly true!'
Was the curé laughing at him? Jean tried another fling.
'Oh, well, anyhow it doesn't mean a thing to me!'

... 'That may be now, my queer little scrap of humanity, but you may feel different later.'
'You shan't get me!'
'It's not a question of my getting you. How could it be?'
'Well, who else could? There's no one else here, is there, except you and Maria?'
The curé said nothing. He seemed to be thinking.[18]

How admirable the reserve, the patience, the understanding, the respect for the personality under his care, the timing of the appropriate moment for instruction.

Abbé Calou has another remarkable quality, the gift to see with the eyes of others, a holy and penetrating charity, a sanctified imagination. The boy tells him of his disillusionment about his mother, and how the roué of an actor was only a man with dyed hair, a bulging paunch, and a grimacing mouth. The gentle abbé said to the boy,

You must tell yourself that in her eyes he represents wit, genius, elegance. To love another person means to see a miracle of beauty which is invisible to the rest of the world.[19]

The abbé insists that passion has blinded his mother to the love she has in her heart for the boy. The boy thrusts the thought away from him, with the outburst, 'I hate her.' The patient priest replies:

'Of course you do, as we all of us *can* hate those we love. Our Lord told us to love our enemies. It is often easier to do that than not to hate those we love.'
'Yes,' said Jean, 'because they can hurt us so frightfully.'[20]

Like Bernanos' country priest, this one also knows that the profoundest fellowship in the world is that of Christ and His sufferings, and that often all we can do for others is to suffer with them, yet what more can we do for Christ's sake? The abbé is meditating:

'One can always suffer for others.' . . . Then he muttered, as though to himself: 'Do I really believe that?' He seemed to have forgotten our presence. 'Yes, I do. What an appalling doctrine it is that acts count for nothing, that no man can gain merit for himself or for those whom he loves. All through the centuries Christians have believed that the humble crosses to which they were nailed on the right and left hand of Our Lord meant something for their own redemption, and for the redemption of those they loved. And then Calvin came and took away that hope. But I have never lost it . . . No,' he said again, 'No!'[21]

He is able to bear all the slings and arrows of outrageous fortune, because in his humility he knows they are deserved and more than deserved. After twelve years of the theological seminary, he bears his disgrace in being sent to the remote heathland of Baluzac, one of the most dreaded livings in the entire diocese.

Study and prayer made up the tale of his days. He decided that he would devote himself entirely to the small flock entrusted to him without looking for any results.[22]

There is no repining even when he can no longer perform this menial but holy task, after Brigitte Pian has reported him as unworthy to hold his office. His life is a living testimony to the Gethsemane attitude: 'Not my will, but Thine be done.' It is, like Bernanos' priest, another case of the imitation of Christ. There is not a mock but a profound humility in him, that is the true mark of sainthood. Even when he is refused the right to offer the sacrifice of the Mass, through the hypocrite's reporting of him, his diary shows how utterly fair he is to her and less than fair to himself.

'Both of us,' he writes, 'she ruled by her reason, I by my feelings, have been inclined to believe that it is our duty to interfere in the destinies of those around us.'[23]

Himself he describes as

God's very useless, nay, his sometimes actively interfering servant.[24]

He sees that his official degradation is a fitting state for a priest:

I now stand in the presence of my God, as naked, as much stripped of all merit, as utterly defenceless as a man can well be. Perhaps it is the state in which those of us should be whose profession it is—if I may so express myself—to be virtuous. It is almost inevitable that the professionally virtuous should hold exaggerated ideas of the importance of their actions, that they should constitute themselves the judges of their own progress in excellence, that, measuring themselves by the standards of those around them, they should be made slightly giddy by the spectacle of their own merits.[25]

He preached and practiced himself first what he advocated in pain to others. And this profound humility is linked with the Infinite's capacity for understanding, pity, and forgiveness.

Each one of us, he had said, has his own peculiar destiny, and it is, perhaps, one of the secrets of the compassionate Justice which watches over us, that there is no universally valid law by which human beings are to be assessed. Every man inherits his own past. For that he is to be pitied, because he carries through life a load made up of the sins and merits of his forbears to an extent which it is beyond our power to grasp. He is free to say yes or no when God's love is offered to him, but which of us can claim the right to judge what it is that influences his choice? [26]

Finally, it is the acceptance of the forgiveness of Christ which transforms the Pharisee woman herself. The last paragraph of this religious masterpiece reads:

In the evening of her life, Brigitte Pian had come to the knowledge that it is useless to play the part of a proud servitor eager to impress his master by a show of readiness to repay his debts to the last farthing. It had been revealed to her that our Father does not ask us to give a scrupulous account of what merits we can claim. She understood at last that it is not deserts that matter but our love.[27]

So lucid a book is its own commentary and it would be as impertinent as it is unnecessary to emphasize the morals and the counsels, which are translucent, and point—like the abbé himself—to the Light of the World.

3. Graham Greene

The brilliant young writer of fear stories, who gloried in the mysterious and the macabre, was announced as a Catholic writer in a study of juvenile delinquency in imaginative form. *Brighton Rock* (1938)[28] was a study not only of the Hell of violence that is gangsterdom, but of a future Hell as well. The liberals were horrified in the progressive era to find so convinced a believer in original sin. Pinkie (the young gangster) of the tenements in a decaying English seaside resort, conversing with his pathetic, frightened but loyal girl friend, Rosie, brought a new dimension into the novel. This snatch of their conversation on Catholicism is typical:

[Pinkie:] 'I don't take any stock in religion. Hell—it's just there. You don't need to think of it—not before you die.'
'You might die sudden.'
He closed his eyes under the bright empty arch, and memory floated up imperfectly into speech. 'You know what they say—"Between the stirrup and the ground, he something sought and something found." '
'Mercy.'
'That's right: Mercy.'
'It would be awful though,' she said slowly, 'if they didn't give you time.' She turned her cheek onto the chalk towards him and added, as if he could help her: 'That's what I always pray. That I don't die sudden.'
'I don't,' he said.[29]

The flat, conventional world of the novel, was invaded by the depth of Hell and the astonishing heights of grace. Human actions had abiding consequences.

The technique of Greene was brilliant also. An expert in describing the sensations of fear and inevitability in a pursuit of evil by justice (of the criminal by the police), now God was the invisible but inexorable Hunter, as in Mauriac whom he so much admires.

The sense of the lost innocence of the world since the Fall is subtly conveyed in the use of symbols of decadence: peeling walls, spiders, the crude aphrodisiacs of the modern world, the artificial fairy-lights on the pier in a Brighton that was once a center for the aristocrats but is now a place where the *nouveaux riches* gyrate in neon-lit hotels and where the masses disport themselves on day-trips in a smaller English equivalent of Coney Island. In Africa *(The Heart of the Matter)* the symbols are the mosquitoes, the frenzied drinking, the cockroaches that are killed to make intervals in boredom. In Mexico *(The Lawless Roads* and *The Power and the Glory)* it is the vultures, the golden-toothed smiles which enable seedy dentists to make a living, the churches converted to secular use, the superstitions of the Indians which are testimony to a degenerate Christianity, and the ruins of past civilizations that proclaim to the insignificant contemporaries that there was a time when men believed.

No man can write more sparely, tautly, telegrammatically, and yet suggest such overtones and undertones of meaning. *Brighton Rock* has two outstanding examples of the conversation with the *double entendre*. Once, when Pinkie is luring Spicer to his death, Spicer speaks of escaping from Brighton to a convivial inn in Nottingham and settling down; Pinkie can use the same words and laconically refer to the escape of death. Then when Ida is talking to her casual lover, she can interpret his perfectly simple remarks as bawdy innuendoes. Moreover,

Greene can freight his sentences in a remarkable way with a sense of determinism, of inexorability—in brief, of a supernatural providence, like that 'compassionate Justice' of which Mauriac writes.

In 1938 Greene was commissioned to write a book on the religious situation in Mexico. The result was *The Lawless Roads* in which he showed how the Catholic Church in Mexico was persecuted and how, although religious services were forbidden, the people continued to honor the God they were prohibited from worshiping publicly. To be a priest in such an atheistic land was to be a hunted man. And paradox of paradoxes, the hunted man is the instrument of the Invisible Hunter, God. Such Greene believed, in a growingly materialistic world, the man of God would have to be. Mexico is, for him, the prelude to the world situation everywhere. Hence the apocalyptic urgency with which he writes.

Greene has a profound recognition of the importance of worship—corporate worship—for the Christian life, which appears in neither Bernanos nor Mauriac to my knowledge. Even the gaudy and ornate have their function in beautifying the lives of the peasants. Thus he describes the Templo del Carmen in San Luis:

I went into the Templo del Carmen, as the dark dropped, for Benediction. To a stranger like myself, it was like going home—a language I could understand—*Ora pro nobis*. The Virgin sat on an extraordinary silver cloud like a cabbage with the Infant in her arms above the altar; all along the walls horrifying statues with musty purple robes stood in glass coffins; and yet it was home. One knew what was going on. Old men came plodding in in dungarees and bare feet, tired out with work, and again I thought: how could one grudge them the gaudy splendour of the giltwork, the incense, the distant immaculate figure on the cloud? The candles were lit, and suddenly little electric lights sprayed out all over the Virgin's head. Even if it were all untrue and there was no God, surely life was happier with the enormous supernatural promise than with the petty social fulfilment, the tiny passion and the machine-made furniture.[30]

Greene was greatly impressed and humbled by the way the tired and exhausted poor after a day's back-breaking work were ready to undertake mortifications in their worship. Again the temptation to cite his vivid writing cannot be resisted. The scene is the Cathedral when Mass is celebrated in an area where it is barely tolerated:

And then you go into the cathedral for Mass—the peasants kneel in their blue dungarees and hold out their arms, minute after minute, in the attitude of crucifixion; an old woman struggles on her knees up the stone floor towards the altar; another lies full length with her forehead on the stones. A long day's work is behind but the mortification goes on. This is the atmosphere of the *stigmata*, and you realise suddenly that perhaps *this* is the population of heaven—these aged, painful, and ignorant faces: they are human goodness . . . You would say that life itself for these was mortification enough: but like saints they seek the only happiness in their lives and squeeze out from it a further pain.[31]

He was to make 'Tabasco with every church destroyed, and Chiapas, where the Mass was forbidden'[32] the scene for his brilliant study of the whisky priest in *The Power and the Glory* which appeared in 1940, a year after the publication of his pilgrimage to Mexico.

The theme of *The Power and the Glory* (1940) is a modern version of the book of Jonah, as man's attempt to evade God and God's pursuit of him. The hunted Catholic priest of Elizabethan days, so finely re-created by another Catholic novelist, Evelyn Waugh in his *Edmund Campion*, reappears, as it were in Mexican guise. Its subtlety lies in Greene's recognition that this man of clay, this earthiest of earthen vessels, is also a testimony to the living God. Even in his fear, as he goes shaking to his death at the hands of the commissar's soldiery, he is a martyr to the Christian faith. (How cleverly Greene contrasts the reality with the story of the plaster saint and marionette of perfection that the Catholic mother is reading about to her children!) Here indeed is God's plenty and we shall only be able to gather a few scraps from this bountiful feast for comment.

By way of interpretation it is interesting to read the exposition of François Mauriac in a remarkable tribute he pays to Graham Greene:

The power and the glory of the Father burst forth in the Mexican curate who loves alcohol too much and who gets one of his parishioners pregnant. A type so common and mediocre that his mortal sins call forth only derision and a shrugging of the shoulders and he knows it. What this extraordinary book shows us is, if I dare say so, the utilization of sin by Grace.[33]

More than this, the Passion is re-enacted again about this derelict first as a meaningless rite which he celebrates with no personal sacrifice, then at the last he sacrifices himself, sees nothing worthy in his act only a necessity laid on him by his ordination. Mauriac is particularly penetrating in his realization of the apocalyptic dimension in Greene:

We feel [he says] it is that hidden presence of God in an atheistic world, that subterranean flowing of Grace which dazzles Graham Greene much more than the majestic façade which the temporal Church still erects above the peoples. If there is a Christian whom the crumbling of the visible Church would not disturb, it is, indeed that Graham Greene whom I heard at Brussels, evoking, before thousands of Belgian Catholics, and in the presence of a dreaming apostolic nuncio, the last Pope of a totally dechristianized Europe, standing in line at the commissary, dressed in spotted gabardine, and holding in his hand, on which still shone the Fisherman's ring, a cardboard valise.[34]

In short, Greene lets us see the new Church of the catacombs in this novel which may be a transcript of the powerlessness and glory of a purified Body of Christ.

Notice that everywhere God is visible only to the eyes of faith, which penetrate spiritual reality behind material phenomena. The American title of the book, later withdrawn, suggests this: *The Labyrinthine Ways*, as it also evokes the figure of Christ, like the Francis Thompson poem, *The Hound of Heaven*, from which it is a quotation. The stranger introduced in the dentist's waiting room, 'the black question-mark', is the priest—a symbol of hidden Grace beneath the shabbiness of clothes and character. The stranger who knocks at the door at the end of the novel, when it seems all priests are dead and God is left without witness in Mexico, reveals himself as another man of God in mufti.

The second chapter brings the motley crew of prisoners before the lieutenant of police. Some are fined for drunkenness, others for defacing election posters, but one man's crime is witness, his charge being that he was 'found wearing a holy medal hidden under his shirt.' Even books of piety can only be smuggled through the customs if they have covers which in their glossiness and titles purport to be of violent sensuality. The wanted man, who appears in the photograph in the police headquarters, is not the kind of priest you would imagine pitting himself against the police state, for he is shown as a complacent young man at a family gathering after the girls had received their first communion. 'You could imagine him petted with small delicacies . . . He sat there plump, with protuberant eyes, bubbling with harmless feminine jokes.' And, 'you could read into a smudgy photograph a well-shaved, well-powdered jowl much too developed for his age. The good things of life had come too early—the respect of his contemporaries, a safe livelihood. The trite religious word upon the tongue, the joke to ease the way, the ready acceptance of other people's homage . . . a happy man.'[35] As we read we shall inevitably compare the later development of the priest who, hunted though he is, be-

lieves in the goodness of everyone but himself, no longer moral
and conscious of his virtue but driven on by religious duty. All
these are symbols, and many more are scattered through the
novel, of 'Godhead here in hiding'—as G. M. Hopkins called the
Catholic Mass.

Even atheism holds an unforgettable memory of a religion
that was; its desperate desire to wipe out all records is also a
witness to the hidden God.

The lieutenant walked home through the shuttered town. All his life
had lain there: the Syndicate of Workers and Peasants had once been a
school. He had helped to wipe out that unhappy memory. The whole
town was changed: the cement playground up the hill near the cemetery
where iron swings stood like gallows in the moony darkness was the site
of the cathedral. The new children would have new memories: nothing
would ever be as it was. There was something of a priest in his intent
observant walk—a theologian going back over the errors of the past to
destroy them again.[36]

The priest, however he has degenerated, is still the elect one—
God's marked man and victim. This he affirms to Coral Fellows,
who from humanitarian reasons, being a foreigner and a Protestant, is his temporary protector. She asks him why he doesn't
just give himself up to the police. The priest said:

There's the pain. To choose pain like that—it's not possible. And it's my
duty not to be caught.

Coral suggests that he would no longer be in danger if he re-
nounced his faith. He said:

It's impossible. There's no way. I am a priest. It's out of my power.

She listened intently and commented:

Like a birth-mark.

Yes, the 'wanted man' of the political police, is also and more significantly God's 'marked man.'[37]

Greene shows that the priest's failure is a failure of discipline: the result of innumerable surrenders. First went the days of abstinence; then the regular reading of his breviary. Then the stone altar required for proper celebration of the Mass was dropped, as too heavy and dangerous to carry with him. There were moral failures: the pregnancy and the constant anodyne of drink. One day, he thought, the rubble of his failures would entirely choke up the source of grace. Yet, damned as he believes himself to be, the spark of grace is shown in his love for his bitter bastard daughter, Brigida. For this hard-faced, unloving child he prays:

O God give me any kind of death—without contrition, in a state of sin— only save the child.[38]

Even this prayer is imperfect, he knows, for he should love every child of God as he does this child.

This sense of charity blossoms in the priest when he is put in the town prison for being in possession of illicit liquor. A pious woman is incarcerated there in the common one-chamber jail. She is criticizing the hole-in-a-corner lovers. The priest answers her:

Saints talk about the beauty of suffering. Well, we are not saints, you and I. Suffering to us is just ugly. Stench and crowding and pain. *That* is beautiful in that corner—to them.

In the long night the priest meditates:

When you visualized a man or a woman carefully, you could always begin to feel pity ... that was a quality God's image carried with it ... when you saw the lines at the corners of the eyes, the shape of the mouth, how the hair grew, it was impossible to hate. Hate was just a failure of the imagination.[39]

He is released and continues his fearful pilgrimage from village to village. Sodden as he may be with whisky, he is not sodden with delusions about himself or human beings. An old prattling woman is risking the lives of the other secret penitents who have come to confess to him, and she is forever talking about her own goodness. The priest says abruptly,

'I'm not interested in your fish supply or in how sleepy you are at night . . . remember your real sins.'
'But I'm a good woman, father,' she squeaked at him in astonishment.
'Then what are you doing here keeping away the bad people?'
He said: 'Have you any love for anyone but yourself?'
'I love God, father,' she said haughtily. He took a quick look at her in the light of the candle burning on the floor—the hard old raisin eyes under the black shawl—another of the pious—like himself.
'How do you know? Loving God isn't any different from loving a man—or a child. It's wanting to be with Him, to be near Him.' He made a hopeless gesture with his hands.
'It's wanting to protect Him from yourself.' 40

The last drawn-out scene of the novel begins when the half-caste, who the priest knows is a traitor, calls him to the death-bed of the American gangster—and this when he has reached the frontier and is making his escape. He goes because it is his duty to give absolution. He sees and speaks the truth with burning honesty. The miserable half-caste, speaking of the dying gangster, wheedles:

'He's dying and you and I wouldn't like to have on our conscience what that man . . .'
'We shall be lucky if we haven't worse.'
'What do you mean, father?'
The priest said, 'He's only killed and robbed. He hasn't betrayed his friends.'
'Holy Mother of God, I've never . . .'
'We both have,' the priest said.41

The gangster refused the absolution that had cost such a long, arduous and perilous journey. The priest himself who wants to receive pardon before he dies, and can only get it from the married priest José, ironically, is refused that consolation. The last kindness he receives is from the lieutenant of police in the cell: it is the anodyne of brandy, so much less comforting than absolution would have been. Yet even in his misery it is of his little daughter that he thinks, rather than of his own certain damnation.

He felt only an immense disappointment because he had to go to God empty-handed, with nothing done at all.[42]

The end is very ordinary. It is seen from the window of the dentist's room, and the disreputable dentist watches it while he is dealing with the trivial pain of the chief of police whose teeth are being filled.

The officer stepped aside, the rifles went up, and the little man suddenly made jerky movements with his arms. He was trying to say something: what was the phrase they were always supposed to use? That was routine, too, but perhaps his mouth was too dry, because nothing came out except a word that sounded more like 'Excuse.' The crash of the rifles shook Mr. Trench . . . Then there was a single shot . . . and the little man was a routine heap beside the wall—something unimportant which had to be cleared away.[43]

Yet the legend is already ballooning, as the pious Catholic mother embroiders the facts with her idealistic fancies.

'Yes, He was one of the martyrs of the Church.'
'He had a funny smell,' one of the little girls said.
'You must never say that again,' the mother said.
'He may be one of the saints.'

The boy wonders if anyone managed to soak some of his blood in a handkerchief as a holy relic. The mother says:

'I think if your father will give me a little money, I shall be able to get a
relic.'
'Does it cost money?'
'How else can it be managed? Everyone can't have a piece.'[44]

The priest died believing that he was the last priest in Mexico
who heard confessions and celebrated the Mass. Yet the novel
ends with the boy opening the door to the insistent knock of a
stranger at night.

'If you would let me in,' the man said with an odd frightened smile, and
suddenly lowering his voice he said to the boy,
'I am a priest.'
'You?' the boy exclaimed.
'Yes,' he said gently, 'My name is Father—' But the boy had already
swung the door open and put his lips to his hand before the other could
give himself a name.'[45]

Surely the meaning of the ending of the novel is that the
nameless priests do not matter as personalities, they are merely
the human instruments of the living God? Like all the saints
they say, 'I must decrease, and He must increase.' These anonymous saints and martyrs, dramatic or undramatic, maintain the
labyrinthine tasks of the hidden but providential God even in
this apparently abandoned world of materialism and atheism.
The generations come and go, but the task of the priest continues—in or out of the catacombs—to witness to the strange,
persistently seeking love of God, and to mediate his grace and
apply it to the souls of men in the confessional and in the Mass
and in all relationships. For Bernanos, for Mauriac, as for
Greene, as, indeed, had been the case with St. Augustine, the
priest is the unbaying beagle of the invisible Hunter God.

V

Pilgrims, Not Strangers

THE Protestant missionary has undoubtedly received rough treatment in the novels of the twentieth century. Somerset Maugham's well-known short story *Rain* (also dramatized and made into a film) contrasts the prostitute without any pretence even to respectability and the lecherous hypocrisy of the medical missionary who always has the Bible on his lips. A. J. Cronin, like Maugham a medical man by profession, in his novel *Grand Canary* repeats the same theme, with few variations, to the obbligato of a harmonium. By now the slander has become a stereotype. The Protestant missionary is an interfering busybody who considers his own superficial and compromising religion superior to the ancient and satisfying faiths of so-called primitive peoples. He is humorless, a kill-joy whose aim is to replace unaffected natural joy with a cringing fear of Hell. He evokes not the sacrificial ideal of the Master of his religion, Christ, but a sanctimonious pietism that bespeaks superiority not humility. He is as ignorant of culture as he is of geography. He is, worst of all, a repressed man and the pent-up volcano will erupt in fornication.

The Catholic missionary has received preferential treatment, largely because of the widespread popularity of the novel (and also of the film) *The Keys of the Kingdom* in which Cronin, then a convert to Roman Catholicism, depicted the heroism of a Scottish priest, Father Chisholm, who spent the best years of his life as a China missionary. An important but subsidiary figure is that of an American Methodist medical missionary, and this represents a partial reparation for the caricature of Protestant missions Cronin had given in *Grand Canary*.

Two questions arise in connection with the poor showing that the Protestant missionary makes in modern fiction. The first is: Is this deserved? For myself I find it very hard to believe that the charge of hypocrisy can fairly be leveled against this class of men and women who in many cases were among the most accomplished and dedicated people of their time, and had sacrificed home-ties for alienation and poverty, and represented in Protestantism those second-milers of consecration—the parallels of the monastic and mendicant orders of the Catholic Church. Their temptations to superiority might have been greater than for the home ministry, but the zeal and dedication were also greater. I cannot find any evidence of hypocrisy in the lives of Livingstone and Moffat in Africa, to take two conspicuous examples who lived very much in the Victorian public eye. I might indeed suspect that in the iconoclastic zeal of some nineteenth-century missionaries there was a tendency to regard the people of non-Christian religions as heathens and to attempt to erase their old beliefs and customs. But even here (and it should be remembered that both the comparative study of religions and social anthropology are modern—specifically, late nineteenth-century—developments), the evidence does not point all in the same direction.

In the South Seas, the area where Maugham's story is located, the most outstanding nineteenth-century Protestant missionary was the Scotsman, James Chalmers. Yet of him, another novelist, no less than Robert Louis Stevenson, who was exiled to that part of the world for his health and came to know the natives well, wrote most glowingly. His testimonial, quite un-

solicited, may be read in *Vailima Letters*[1], where he writes of
Dr. Chalmers:

a man that took me fairly by storm for the most attractive, simple, brave,
and interesting man in the whole Pacific . . . He is quite a Livingstone
card.

Such a man obviously struck a novelist as being both cultivated
and a man of integrity. What is even more apposite, however,
is to read what Stevenson has to say about the local emissaries
of the London Missionary Society, Congregationalists. For
Maugham, it will be remembered, makes a great point that the
kill-joy Davidson has stamped out the native dancing. Quite
casually, as if it were unworthy of particular notice, Stevenson
states: 'Mr. Clarke the missionary and his wife assisted at a
native dance.' This entry in the diary was made in 1890, almost
twenty years before *Rain* appeared (1919).

The second question that needs to be raised is this: Is there
any evidence of a change of heart on the part of novelists in
their treatment of Protestant missionaries? One swallow does
not make a summer, nor does one novel symbolize a change of
attitude. Nonetheless, in *Cry, the Beloved Country*, Alan Paton's splendid modern novel of race relationships in the griev-
ously divided and ironically named Union of South Africa,
there is a profile of an Episcopalian or Church of England missionary, which is a long-delayed tribute to the Protestant missionary. What makes this brief reference all the more significant
is that it is believed that Alan Paton has in mind here his old
Johannesburg friend, Father Trevor Huddleston, who has written his own testament in the moving book *Naught for your
Comfort*.

The fact remains that major novelists, whether Catholic or
Protestant, have given very little consideration in fiction to the
role of the missionary. The deserved tribute is all the more

deplorable in being delayed because the modern developments of missions are increasingly indigenous, and away from 'foreign missions.'* Perhaps the novelists of the future will concentrate on the reconciling figures in a multi-racial society, though these will be priests and ministers and sacrificial laity. But this is the major problem of our age, and demands religious literary treatment. And of this genre of the future, Alan Paton's *Cry, the Beloved Country* and its successor, in which no clerical character appears, *Too late the Phalarope*, are the only distinguished examples. The field has been left too long to the humanists,[2] who have excluded the dimensions of sin and grace in the consideration of what is to them only a social problem, not a theological one.

These considerations mean that we should turn with particular concern to the few novels on this theme.

1. W. Somerset Maugham

Rain is a short story of only some thirty-nine pages, yet the impression its sharply delineated characters and incidents leave is a lasting, if unpleasant, one. In fact, it is much more vivid than Cronin's treatment of a similar theme—with an extra dimension of a finer love for contrast—despite the fact that *Grand Canary* is eight times its length. *Rain* tells the sordid story of a Calvinistic medical missionary who tries to run a prostitute out of his missionary territory as a menace to the natives, only to commit fornication with her, and afterwards shoot himself.

Physically large, the offending doctor and evangelist, Dr. Davidson has a petty little soul. He and his wife, who should be the humble servants of Christ, are snobs. He refuses to mix

---

* 'Foreign' missionaries in the lands of the Younger Churches are few and termed 'fraternal workers.'

with what he considers to be riffraff on the ship. Maugham's chief objections are as much aesthetic as they are moral. He thus describes Mrs. Davidson:

Her face was long, like a sheep's, but she gave no impression of foolishness, rather of extreme alertness; she had the quick movements of a bird. The most remarkable thing about her was her voice, high, metallic, and without inflection; it fell on the ear with a hard monotony, irritating to the nerves like the pitiless clamour of the pneumatic drill.[3]

The lady takes a prurient delight in what she is supposed to abhor. It is a very cowardly sense of delicacy she shows in telling another doctor's wife to relate to her husband some of the details of the marriage customs of the natives! She has all the gloom of the Calvinist, coupled with a sense of superiority as one of the elect.

There was not, in Mrs. Davidson's opinion, a single good girl to be found in any of the villages. She reminded the visitors of the nuisance of mosquitoes and the probable persistence of rain, and all in a very knowing and irritating manner.

Both Dr. Davidson and his wife are kill-joys, blue-law Puritans with a fascination for what they condemn. Their first decision on reaching the islands was to stamp out the native dances. They thought the constructive solution to the sexual problem was to make every boy of ten years of age wear a pair of trousers! (This is a very old gibe, indeed. One is surprised that Maugham should revive this chestnut.)

For a missionary Dr. Davidson was a singularly morose and sullen man, who considered affability a duty and with whom intimacy of mind was impossible. He is a long, lean cadaverous man, a fanatic, and he has the courage of the fanatic's faith. He will face the breakers and even the storms in his canoe quite fearlessly to take his medicines and the Gospel to the remoter islands. When his wife remonstrates with him, he answers,

How can I ask the natives to put their trust in the Lord if I am afraid to do so myself? . . . And do you think the Lord is going to abandon me when I am on His business? [4]

Here the caricature dissolves to reveal the truth. It was the magnificent Coillard in South Africa who said, 'I am immortal until my work is done.' At least Maugham glimpsed here the iron in the will that the doctrine of election and predestination gives to those who hold it.

But Davidson has also the defects of that pitiless creed. There is a hard, systematic legalism about him, even a vindictiveness disguised as justice, which he is too ready to equate with Divine justice. The victory that he and his wife were most proud of was their terrorizing of a Danish trader who was sexually and alcoholically indulgent, until he lost his shop and came groveling before them. It is clear that these sadists have made God in their own image, and herein there is an implicit warning. Just as a degenerate Calvinism made God a cruel and arbitrary judge and sanctioned vengefulness and witch-hunting in human affairs, so does a febrile emotionalism turn him into 'our Grandfather who art in Heaven,' as an image of an amoral sentimentalism. The holiness and the love of God ought never to be divided.

It is significant that Davidson is also a tremendous sentimentalist. His tear-streaming prayers and orgies of emotionalism are his ultimate undoing. This man who is stern to others and weak in himself—his sternness masks repression—actually seduces the prostitute who sincerely desires to be converted by him. The sardonic ending of the story comes with Sadie's outburst:

You men! You filthy dirty pigs! You're all the same, all of you. Pigs! Pigs! [5]

It is worth discussing an otherwise insignificant story for two reasons. First, because this has become the stereotype of

the repressed man of God in modern literature. The significance of this was pointed out by Graham Greene in his *Journey without Maps*, in asserting that Maugham 'has done more
than anyone to stamp the idea of the repressed prudish man of
God on the popular imagination. *Rain* has impressed the image
of Mr. Davidson over the missionary field.'

The second reason for an interest in *Rain* is that the normally
tolerant and even clinical attitude of Doctor Maugham is set
aside whenever he deals with clerical characters. His deep aversion to clergymen is displayed in another short story *The Ver-
ger*, in his early play *Loaves and Fishes*, and most importantly
in his great novel *Of Human Bondage* (1915). We can probe
the roots of the aversion to the parson in this novel because it is
largely autobiographical,[6] being concerned with a sensitive boy
who was adopted by an Anglican clergyman and who rejected
the career in the Church planned for him. It is not the animus
that is important, but the reasons for it.

To enumerate the failings of the Rev. William Carey as re-
counted in *Of Human Bondage* is to produce a catalogue that
reads like an anti-clerical tirade article of the Rationalist Press
in its most dogmatic early twentieth-century phase. He is, of
course, aesthetically repulsive. That can be guaranteed in any
character this novelist dislikes. The Vicar of Blackstable is short
and stout and—symbol of his hypocrisy—wears his hair long in
the attempt to cover the basic baldness. That this is an exaggerated characterization is suggested by the fact that he has
unusual deficiencies for the cloth, being almost devoid of
vocabulary, and a purchaser of second-hand books which he
does not read! He is utterly selfish—the antithesis of the ethics
he is supposed to follow. He expected his ward and nephew,
who has a club-foot, to walk from the station to the vicarage,
although he could easily have afforded a cab. He is inconsiderate
to his wife: the stove in the hall is lighted only when he has a

cold; his wife and nephew can catch cold while he has a fire in his study to facilitate sermon-preparation. His overbearing attitude to his curate, whom he regards as a menial not a colleague, is suggested in a casual description of the furniture of the hearthside in the living room.

Mr. Carey was making up the fire when Philip came in, and he pointed out to his nephew that there were two pokers. One was large and bright and polished and unused, and was called the Vicar; and the other which was much smaller and had evidently passed through many fires, was called the Curate.[7]

Since his salary does not permit both himself and his wife to take holidays abroad, he goes off by himself. The clergyman's miserliness and sanctimoniousness are admirably caught in the following incident. When they are seating the small nephew at table, the maid produces a Bible to add to the chair's height, and a prayer-book. The good, honest, simple Mrs. Carey is rather shocked by this treatment of the Holy Book.

'Oh William, he can't sit on the Bible,' she remonstrates and begs the Vicar to get some other books from his study. Considering the question for an instant, he replies:
'I don't think it matters this once if you put the prayerbook on the top, Mary Ann,' he said. 'The Book of Common Prayer is the composition of men like ourselves. It has no claim to Divine authorship.'

The incident continues:

Philip perched himself on the books, and the Vicar, having said grace, cut off the top of his egg.
'There,' he said, handing it to Philip, 'you can eat my top if you like.'
Philip would have liked an egg to himself, but he was not offered one, so he took what he could . . .
'How did you like that top, Philip?' asked his uncle.
'Very much, thank you.'
'You shall have another one on Sunday afternoon.'[8]

We are not yet at the end of the catalogue of the Vicar's faults. He was intolerant and snobbish and very conscious of the respect due to him, as was shown on the occasion when he had to point out to his overweening church warden 'that parson meant person, that is, the vicar was the person of the parish.' He was, for one who had been presumably bred at an English public school and inculcated in that mixture of classics, cold baths, team spirit, and social superiority, curiously an ignoramus at Latin, and a very poor loser at backgammon. He is also testy and ill-humored.

His wife's death is for him neither a tragedy of bereavement nor an occasion of Christian gratification because she is bound for eternal life; it is merely an inconvenience. The Vicar hopes that her grave will be adorned with more floral tributes than that of a neighboring Vicar's wife's was. When the church warden discusses the matter of the tombstone, the Vicar argues for economy under the pretext of his wife's dislike of ostentation. The church warden suggests that the appropriate Biblical inscription would be, 'With Christ, which is far better.' But the Vicar refuses the suggestion; 'it seemed to cast an aspersion on himself.'[9]

The final obloquy is left for the Vicar's old age. Though the machine is running down, he has a desperate desire to live. Greed for money and for food are his predominating characteristics in this period. What seemed most hideous about his old age and oncoming death was his clinging to life, and his fear of death, when he had always taught others that death was the gateway to life everlasting. This was the ultimate hypocrisy. Philip was so eager for him to die so he might inherit his uncle's legacy that he was sorely tempted to murder him. That, of itself, shows that there was a deep personal hatred against this particular clerical uncle at the most impressionable period of

Maugham's life. Ever since clergymen have made Maugham see black!

The novel, however, is of great value in providing a detailed analysis of loss of faith, which is not entirely explained by the un-Christian behavior of Philip's guardian. It is chiefly Maugham's complaint that Christianity prepares the impressionable boy for a world of superhuman goodness and faith that can perform miracles, which subsequent experience destroys, with a consequent bitter disillusionment. One of his characters is prepared to accept Christianity for its aesthetic values, while denying it any ontological validity. This compassionate eccentric who has a passion for all things Spanish also argues that religion is the best school for morality.

It is like one of those drugs you gentlemen use in medicine which carries another in solution; it is of no efficacy in itself, but enables the other to be absorbed. You take your morality because it is combined with religion; you lose the religion but the morality stays behind.

He argues cogently that 'a man is more likely to be a good man if he has learned goodness through the love of God than through a perusal of Herbert Spencer.'[10] But Philip, presumably Maugham himself, though moved by the appeal is unconvinced. Life is for him a complex maze on which a man can project a pattern, but every philosophy is only the reflex of the philosopher's temperament and has validity only for those who share the same temperament. In any case, it is of no importance but to the man himself and at death ceases to have even that significance. If any generalization can be made about Maugham's attitude to the ministry and to religion it would be this: he is bitter, as Thomas Hardy was bitter, at the loss of a faith that would have given life purpose, but which, it seems, an intelligent man cannot accept because it is a beautiful falsehood, and priests and parsons are its purveyors. Only the slave accepts the 'human bondage' of faith.

2. A. J. Cronin

If Maugham's is the story of a believer turned skeptic, Cronin's is that of a skeptic converted.[11] The skeptical treatment of religion is, as was earlier suggested, a republication of the thesis of *Rain* in his novel *Grand Canary* (1933). Robert Tranter, a Seventh Day Adventist missionary from Trenton, New Jersey, the son of a baker, is Cronin's equivalent for Maugham's Davidson. They share the same characteristics. He has the gift of gab, is emotional in his religion, and views his future charges, the natives, with contempt. He is, however, not taciturn and morose like Davidson, but a great smiler, hand-shaker, and personality-pusher. This makes him an unlovely compound of Davidson and Elmer Gantry. He has a crude and brash outlook:

Personality counts in business anywhere. Good enough. I'll say it counts double in the biggest business deal in life. And that, Sue, is putting over the Word of God.[12]

He is willing to tell his life's story at the drop of a hat.

He, too, is a kill-joy. No smoking or drinking for him. Wine he objects to, women he is addicted to, and if Sankey and Moody be song, he is an enthusiast. His most disgusting characteristic is his hypocrisy. In him it takes the sanctimonious form of mixing religion with lust, and claiming that opportunities for illicit intercourse are providential. Here his knowledge of the Book of Genesis becomes much too handy. He is utterly selfish. His subsequently cowardly, indulgent, and besotted life only proves that there may be original sin, but there are no *original* sins to commit. The novelist's verdict on him is probably that expressed by the lady of easy virtue whose cabin he shared aboard ship:

You're all surface, my saintly friend, and quite hollow inside. You're not a man. You're a fool, a selfish Bible-banging fool, without the backbone of a spider. I'm selfish and know it. But you—you're the most hidebound egoist that ever hummed a psalm-tune. And you think you're a God-sent minister of the Light—Heaven's gift to humanity. You say you're sincere. That's the worst of it. If you were a hypocrite, I might respect you. But you believe you're a saviour. You bound about roaring salvation. Then the moment you're hurt, you begin to snivel.[13]

Since the character is borrowed, and the characterization unconvincing (how could a woman respect a hypocrite more than a merely deluded man, even in a rage?), it is both more charitable and more profitable to turn to Cronin's act of reparation.

The Keys of the Kingdom (1941) is the story of a poor, honest, independent Scots boy, Francis Chisholm, unconventional yet always sincere, who receives almost no recognition from the Catholic Church although he becomes an excellent missionary in China, as contrasted with his schoolboy friend, Anselm Mealey, who has all the superficial graces, and rises to the eminence of a prelate. In narrative interest it surpasses both *The Diary of a Country Priest* and *A Woman of the Pharisees,* but in psychological penetration is inferior to both, yet its theme is the same—'Blessed are the meek.' On the other hand, it has some admirable qualities. It presents a wide range of clerical portraits, missionary and ministerial, including a sectarian 'ranter,' a sympathetic American Methodist medical missionary, and a variety of Catholic priests, sympathetic and unsympathetic, with a vivid profile of a missionary Mother Superior. It breathes a liberal and tolerant Catholicism, which is aware of the splendor and also of the squalor of some of its representatives. It tries hard to be fair to Protestantism, and its discussion of the temptation of the Church as an organization to capitalize on a faith that may become credulity, in the report of a vision of the Virgin that a neurotic girl is supposed to have received, is penetrating and judicious. Above all it is an intelligible and sympathetic account of a modern missionary priest, itself a great rarity.

Its chief defect is that while it is an *ecclesiastical* novel and a good one, it is in no sense a *theological* novel. It is concerned with integrity of morals, with compassion, and service. But it does not penetrate the mystery with the searching categories of Grace and sin, as do Greene, Mauriac, and Bernanos, and its hero, if unrewarded by the Catholic Church, has those qualities that a humanist would recognize, without requiring a supernatural origin for their explanation. It is, therefore, a novel about Christians, but not a distinctively or consistently *Christian* interpretation of human nature and destiny. It oscillates between humanist and Christian perspectives.

It does, however, have some specifically Christian insights. Cronin sees that there is a middle way between Puritanism and licentiousness, and that the difference between lust and love is that between disease and health. Cronin further recognizes that humility is the distinguishing mark of the true priest as pride is of the worldling, and that forgiveness and the desiring to be forgiven is the way back to humility. He knows, too, that faith and courage are as intimately related as cause and effect.

The chief distinction of this novel, however, is found in its central figure, Francis Chisholm, S. J. He has succeeded in making him the symbol of spontaneous and sacrificial love, mirroring the *agape*—the Divine generosity—of the Gospels. Chisholm is superbly contrasted with the successful man of the Church, Anselm Mealey, so that Mealey seems more like a successful man of the world. Mealey has the gift of speech, the future prelate's suavity of manner, the capacity to organize and the accompanying defect of reducing men to statistics. Chisholm is awkward in manner, spontaneous rather than calculating, and has a complete disregard for convention. For him a man or a woman, European or Chinese, is a person of infinite worth for whom Christ died, never a statistic. And when he has to be ready to face martyrdom (from which, in fact, he escapes by a last-minute reprieve), he is unflinching and chiefly concerned to encourage others in the time of trial.

When Chisholm finally returns from China (he has had no sabbaticals or furloughs) he asks for an interview with the bishop of the diocese of his boyhood in the hope that he may be permitted to act as parish priest in his home town. The bishop, the Right Reverend Anselm Mealey, is late for the interview and, despite the fact that he will soon have to leave for a social function, does all the talking. The humble Chisholm is awed by the presence of the successful prelate:

'I feel like an old ragman beside you, Anselm, and that is God's truth,' he remarks. Then, he adds, a little hopefully, 'I hope you're not altogether dissatisfied with my work in Taipan.'

The suave and sleek bishop replies, with a judgment that is self-judgment:

My dear father, your efforts were heroic. Naturally we're a little disappointed with the figures . . . In all your thirty-six years you made less conversions than Father Lawler in five.[14]

The book closes with the inspection of Chisholm's parish by the bishop's right-hand man, Monsignor Sleeth. The complaints of a few parishioners compelled the inquiry. The urbane Sleeth finds that he is lacking in dignity, having watched him making kites for small boys. He is amazed at his heretical tolerance of other faiths, and at his friendship for the Presbyterian minister. He is also disturbed by his eccentricity. But, after a rather unconvincing dream, he is persuaded that this man is a true priest of God, and prays

O Lord, let me learn something from this old man. And, dear Lord. . . .
Don't let me be a bore.[15]

Cronin has given us another portrait of the simple Christian
at odds with a self-seeking world, and also regarded as eccentric
by a conventional and often compromising Church. Chisholm
quite properly bears (although he is a Jesuit) the first name
Francis, the apostle of Christian love and the bridegroom of
Lady Poverty. He is of the same tradition as *le jongleur de
Notre Dame* and Don Camillo, in his Christian simplicity,
spontaneity, and utter dedication to God and man. He is, indeed, the eccentric individualist, the cat that walks by itself.
As his former seminary Rector sees him:

You are the stray cat, Francis, who comes stalking up the aisle when
everyone is yawning their heads off at a dull sermon . . . and quite the
nicest thing about you, my dear boy is this—you haven't got that
bumptious security which springs from dogma rather than from faith.[16]

It is this undogmatic faith of his which makes it possible for him
to respect the agnosticism of a medical friend, who dies in the
attempt to obliterate a plague from Tai-pan. As he is dying the
priest offers him the only comfort he can, but so sensitively.
Tulloch says:

'I still can't believe in God.' Father Francis replied,
'He still believes in you.' The dying man says:
'Don't delude yourself . . . I'm not repentant.' The priest counters:
'All human suffering is an act of repentance.'

In the last silence before the end, Tulloch reached out his
fevered hand from the bedclothes and, as he rested it on the
priest's arm, he said:

Man, I've never loved ye so much as I do now . . . for not trying to bully
me into heaven.[17]

For Father Francis Chisholm men were immortal souls, never ecclesiastical scalps. And that Christian conviction is also a judgment on the statisticmongers of the modern Church in many branches.

3. Alan Paton

For reasons, which were given earlier, the so-called 'foreign missionary' may become a diminishing figure in a world in which the West and its religion are increasingly rejected by the East and in which missionaries themselves speak, not of 'Mission-Fields' but of 'The Younger Churches'; but the problems of racial tensions are more rather than less acute in the twentieth century. One might even risk the generalization that the great problem of the latter nineteenth century was the conflict between Christian ethical norms and the economic order, while in the twentieth century the chief problem is the antagonism between Christian principles and race hatreds and prejudices. It is therefore of the utmost relevance that an important novelist, out of the heart of the interracial complexities of South Africa with its many bitter racialists and its few intrepid Christian and humanist anti-segregationists, should have chosen this theme in his moving novel, *Cry, the Beloved Country* (1948).

While the hero is a social reformer who, ironically, is killed by a member of the people he is trying to uplift, he is moved by Christian impulses and convictions. More important for our purpose, however, is that the author, Alan Paton, gives a sympathetic portrayal of two priests, the Rev. Stephen Kumalo, an African rural priest of the Church of the Province of South Africa (the Anglican or Episcopalian Church) and an English missionary priest of the same Communion, Father Vincent. The understanding and compassionate English priest is a portrayal of Father Trevor Huddleston, a great friend of Paton's, who was a notable priest of the Anglican Community of the Resurrection in Johannesburg. Paton thus seems to be saying that while educational, political, and social amelioration is essential, (and he was himself a teacher and for many years the principal of the Reformatory School for African offenders in Johannesburg), the ultimate reconciliation of racial tensions is to be found in Christian humility, forgiveness, and compassion, which are the gift of Christ, the Reconciler of men with God and with themselves. The constructive meaning of suffering with Christ is 'The Comfort in Desolation,' which is the subtitle of the novel.

Reduced to a fleshless skeleton, the story is that of an old African minister's search for his prodigal son, which causes him to leave his little valley church in Natal for the Babylon of Johannesburg, where industrialization, de-tribalization, and a shoddy imitation of the material aspects of civilization are turning so many of the Africans into prodigals. In the end, after a search that takes him through many aspects of the lives of the city Africans, he finds his son in jail, where he is to be charged with the murder of Jarvis, the social reformer—the two other equally, if not more, guilty accomplices having escaped from justice. The minister also discovers that his own sister has become a prostitute in Johannesburg, the city of Gold, where the African gold miners are not permitted to bring their wives to share their quarters. His brother has become a rabble rouser and critic of the Church in Johannesburg. In Johannesburg old Kumalo is greatly helped by the white priest, with whom he stays (hotels for whites are forbidden to Africans) and who interprets the meaning of suffering constructively. In the end he returns home, saddened but unbroken in faith to find that his great helper is the local white farmer, previously prejudiced in racial matters, whose son Jarvis had been killed by Kumalo's son. Only a profound and mutual and, as Paton believes, supernaturally originating forgiveness could have made this relationship possible. It is in such possibilities of creatively overcoming race tensions that the greatest hope in South Africa lies. It is a novel that avoids the usual dangers of a bitter realism (though it spares nothing in its description of the common decay of European and African moral life) and of a facile sentimentalism (though it shows that Christian love is deeply sacrificial and forgiving in its compassion).

The Rev. Stephen Kumalo is a simple and poorly educated man. His church is no more than a wood-and-iron construction; there are no temptations to wealth here. There might be temptations to prestige and bullying his people. But this humble man is always God's servant, sometimes his bewildered servant, never the master of his flock. He is, of course, in his search for his lost son, the type of God. In the same way Jarvis, sacrificed though a reconciler, is a shadowy type of God's eternal Son, Christ. When Kumalo sets out on the search he and his wife have ten pounds in the savings bank and a little more than twelve pounds that they have set aside for their son's education. This money, earned with the sweat of their brows and saved by much skimping, is immediately used for the great search, for in their estimation human values always predominate over money values—and yet to whom does money mean more than to the honest poor? Yet these savings have to be spent on a journey which—for a simple countryman—is into the anxious frontiers of sophistication and civilization. As the train takes him farther away from the green valleys he loves to the unfamiliar industrial metropolis, his fear mounts. In Paton's own words:

And now the fear back again, the fear of the unknown, the fear of the great city where boys were killed crossing the street, the fear of Gertrude's sickness. Deep down the fear for his son. Deep down the fear of a man who lives in a world not made for him, whose own world is slipping away, dying, being destroyed, beyond any recall.[18]

For reassurance he turned to the pastoral world of the Bible, which alone was real for him. And even there, in his later agony and perturbation, he was to lose his way until the Anglican missionary priest helped him stumblingly to find it again.

The old priest's simplicity means that he trusts everyone and is as easily gulled as his eighteenth-century prototype, Gold-smith's *Vicar of Wakefield*. In his case it is not green spectacles or a sorry nag that is his undoing, but a fellow African who absconds with his pound note after pretending to buy a bus ticket from the depot. His disillusionment deepens when he learns that his sister, who went to seek her husband, has become a prostitute, and that his brother is no longer a business man but a rabble-rousing politician, symptom and channel of African resentment, who says:

What God has not done for South Africa, man must do.[19]

The diagnosis of the racial problem is given in several parts of the novel. A younger African priest, Msimangu, who be-friended old Kumalo, gives his view first:

'My friend, I am a Christian. It is not in my heart to hate a white man. It was a white man who brought my father out of darkness. But you will pardon me if I talk frankly to you. The tragedy is not that things are broken. The tragedy is that they are not mended again. The white man has broken the tribe. And it is my belief—and again I ask you pardon—that it cannot be mended again. But the house that is broken, and the man that falls apart when the house is broken, these are tragic things. That is why children break the law, and old white people are robbed and beaten.' Msimangu continues: 'It suited the white man to break the tribe . . . But it has not suited him to build something in the place of what is broken . . . They are not all so. There are some white men who give their lives to build up what is broken.—But they are not enough . . . They are afraid, that is the truth. It is fear that rules this land.'[20]

The same deep African priest develops his diagnosis more subtly later:

... there is only one thing that has power completely, and that is love. Because when a man loves, he seeks no power, and therefore has power. I see only one hope for our country, and that is when white men and black men, desiring neither power nor money, but desiring only the good of their country, come together to work for it.

Msimangu was grave and silent and then he said somberly,

I have one great fear in my heart, that one day when they are turned to loving, they will find we are turned to hating.[21]

The liberal and intelligent white man, young Jarvis, had been penning his own diagnosis when death struck him. This was even more subtle, as well as profound, in its exploration of the dilemmas in South Africa and the utter contradictions. Its final words are worth pondering, because almost universal in their scope:

The truth is that our civilization is not Christian; it is a tragic compound of great ideal and fearful practice, of high assurance and desperate anxiety, of loving charity and fearful clutching of possessions.[22]

Meanwhile, as time runs out, Paton hopes that Christians will be able to implement their moral imperatives and by a mutual forgiveness increase the healing of the antagonisms.

Father Vincent's role is deserving of consideration—especially when it is realized that behind this fictional character stands Father Trevor Huddleston. As Paton portrays Father Vincent, four characteristics predominate. Like all confessors he is an excellent listener, and never a perfunctory one. He knows when a man has become so numb with grief that no words can comfort him. So profound in his capacity for communication that he can speak as the African pastor wishes him to speak, in parables. This conversation is typical of his method:

—My friend, your anxiety turned to fear, and your fear turned to sorrow. But sorrow is better than fear. For fear impoverishes always, while sorrow may enrich. Kumalo looked at him, with an intensity of gaze that was strange in so humble a man, and hard to encounter.
—I do not know that I am enriched, he said.
—Sorrow is better than fear, said Father Vincent doggedly. Fear is a journey, a terrible journey, but sorrow is an arriving.
—And where have I arrived? asked Kumalo.
—When the storm threatens, a man is afraid for his house, said Father Vincent in that symbolic language that is like the Zulu tongue. But when the house is destroyed, there is something to do. About a storm he can do nothing, but he can rebuild a house.[23]

Father Vincent is also a surgeon of the soul and he now speaks severely, certain that this will best help Kumalo and recall him to his vocation as a priest:

—We spoke of amendment of life, said the white priest. Of the amendment of your son's life. And because you are a priest, this must matter to you more than all else, more even than your suffering and your wife's suffering.
—That is true. Yet I cannot see how such a life can be amended.
—You cannot doubt that. You are a Christian. There was a thief upon the cross.[24]

Finally, Father Vincent is a practical man and knows that hope arises when a man is reminded of his many tasks and duties and of the dependence of others upon him. He is counseled to pray in a severely practical and concrete way which will also be, though this is not mentioned, a way of healing and forgiveness:

Do not pray and think about these things now, there will be other times. Pray for Gertrude, and for her child, and for the girl that is to be your son's wife, and for the child that will be your grandchild. Pray for your wife and for all at Ndotsheni. Pray for the woman and the children that are bereaved. Pray for the soul of him who was killed. Pray for us at the Mission House, and for those at Ezenzelini, who try to rebuild in a place of destruction. Pray for your own rebuilding. Pray for all white people, those who do justice, and those who would do justice if they were not afraid. And do not fear to pray for your son, and his amendment . . . And give thanks where you can give thanks.[25]

When Kumalo would have thanked the rosy-cheeked priest from England, Father Vincent replied,

We do what is in us, and why it is in us, that is also a secret. It is Christ in us, crying that men may be succoured and forgiven, even when He Himself is forsaken.[26]

In the novel Father Vincent is merely a profile, taking up only a chapter, but his outline is so firmly etched that the essential priest is here, and, though of a different Christian Communion, he challenges comparison with Mauriac's Abbé Calou, with due allowance for the much briefer treatment.

Much could be written of the poetic quality of the novel and its Biblical simplicity and profundity of speech, of the deliberate inversion of the order of the words to suggest in English the dignity of the Zulu language, of the contrasts between the village and primitive and the city and sophisticated environments, were our concern with the technique of the novel rather than the meaning. Its ultimate meaning is the necessity for reconciliation between the races, which are necessary to each other for the establishment of a harmonious society that will reflect the variety of the gifts of God to men—the example, incentive, and power for compassion and forgiveness that Christ the Reconciler shows and gives. It is only a superficial though obvious and easy judgment that would imply that the white man has all the giving to do and the black man all the receiving. But civilization is not merely European and Western, though its latest phase has been so. The Africans themselves have, as Paton's novel shows us, their own important human gifts to provide. They are a marvelously patient people, whose contentment should shame the neurotic greed characteristic of so many in the West. They have a profound concern for the young and the old, and will share their food and shelter with the widows and fatherless in their affliction, however little of this world's goods of their own they have. Here again their social solidarity and generosity should make Western individualists uncomfortable in their isolation and atomism. They have a rich capacity for joy, as shown in their singing and dancing. They have a very gracious courtesy, grave and tender. Their eye for color is exotic, as may be seen in their tribal decoration and on the lintel posts of their beehive huts in their kraals. And while only the antiquarian anthropologist (of whom there are few left) and the sentimental segregationist want them to live in their reserves and their poor city 'locations,' Paton has shown that detribalization has gone too far. They must be integrated in a new Western society in which their human qualities will be needed even more than at present along with the skills that they have proved they can learn when the white man gives them their opportunity.

It is not the least of Paton's distinctions that he has provided a moving sociological document, which is a human document and at the same time a theological document, a Christian interpretation of racial tensions and of the spirit by which they can be overcome. In the same volume he has also supplied an account of a simple yet dignified Zulu pastor and of a clever but humble English missionary priest, which helps to wipe out the sneers of Somerset Maugham. It was altogether typical of Paton that his

next novel, *Too Late the Phalarope*, should attempt to deal sympathetically and understandingly with the problem of the
Afrikaner, the other and larger part of the white minority in
South Africa which is exacerbating the racial problem, apart
from certain distinguished exceptions. He seems to have made
it his concern to apply the Biblical adage to tell the truth in
love.[27]

VI

Community Leaders

THE most recent development in the role of the minister is that of community leader or director of community life. It is an important development since it conceives of the ministry in relation to man's social, educational, and therapeutic needs, thus giving the ministry a direct relevance to the community. It is also a potentially dangerous development, since the minister may become no more than a social reformer, an educationalist, an amateur psychologist or psychotherapist, a cultural leader, or an executive, whose primary preaching, liturgical, and pastoral responsibilities—in the traditional sense—may be submerged. Even if the community which he directs avoids, in being other-directed, the smugness of a religious club it may cease to be, as it were, upper-directed.

There was always the possibility within Protestantism that the minister might become, in addition to his primary function as preacher and teacher of the Word of God, a community director. Generally a married man, and therefore no celibate, he shared the family responsibilities and privileges of most of his congregation, and as a result was closer to them than a celibate priest could be; though, of course, many celibate priests have had the time and freedom from family responsibility to be real fathers to their flocks. Furthermore, with Luther's teaching that God was to be served, not so much in a special calling, like the ministry of the Word, but in all vocations, a great incentive was given to service in the community of the wider world. No longer was there a first-class Christianity available only to monks, friars, celibate priests, and nuns, and a second-class Christianity available as a substitute, and a sorry one, for the married in the world. Henceforth in Protestantism one was either a good Christian in the world, or a bad Christian in the world, never a Christian withdrawn from the world. Thus for Protestants the term 'religious community' has never been limited to the monastic and mendicant orders, as in Roman Catholicism; the religious community is the body of the faithful, gathered not only in the church for worship, but gathered in the family or scattered in the world, where the father, presiding at family prayers, or with his workmen, is also the father-in-God.

The fullest development of the conception of the minister as director of the community had to await nineteenth-and twentieth-century developments, however. This can be viewed with special clarity on the American scene, where the minister had no secure and settled status, such as an ecclesiastical establishment was able to give Anglican clergy in England or Lutherans in Germany, or Calvinists in Switzerland. The voluntary pluralism by which religion was organized in the United States within almost every State within a generation after the end of the Revolution, meant that ministers of every denomination had to rely entirely on their own congregations for financial support, and this, in turn, required the congregations to be 'live' organizations and the ministers 'live wires.' So that the American minister has almost always been an able organizer.

In the extraordinary mobility of the population in the nineteenth century the minister had a special significance. Industrialization meant that the villages became depopulated as first men and soon afterwards their families flocked to the towns and mushrooming cities in search of better wages, and often as the only means of getting employment. In their bewilderment in a new environment, they turned hopefully to the church as a source of spiritual security and greatly needed friendship. Similarly, the flood of immigrants from Europe, especially in the latter half of the century, required the services of ministers to integrate them into American life. But the supreme need for the minister as organizer was seen on the edges of the moving westward frontier. In that new and unfamiliar world, where honest families sought for new land or prospected for minerals and where dishonest and unprincipled men sought their easy victims, the Methodist and Baptist preachers were often the only personal centers of the small and mobile communities. This was inevitable, for as ministers they were men of integrity, really trustworthy in a group of strangers. Furthermore, they were men of some education and they had a personal 'charisma' which bespoke authority. They lived simply and roughly and were approachable. Such men, as can easily be documented in Cartwright's diary,[1] were the nexus of the community, acting as evangelists, also as family and community counselors, and medical aides. In that changing world, the Methodist itinerant preacher and the Baptist farmer-preacher were unchallenged as the directors of their communities, and in the mid-West and South their churches are to this day the most influential.

As the century developed, however, currents in the world of thought were also modifying the conception of the minister. Indirectly, the nineteenth-century world-pond was to ripple to the effects of the giant stones thrown into it by Karl Marx and Charles Darwin, as the twentieth century was to be influenced by Sigmund Freud's rock throwing. Some long-term effects of Marx included the development of the 'Social Gospel' and the sensitizing of the social conscience to the gross inequities of the economic system, and the need to create institutional churches for the poor, where soup-kitchens, employment bureaus, language classes for immigrants, savings-banks, and instructions in various skills supplemented the traditional ministries of the Church, especially in the great cities such as New York. As the new evolutionary hypothesis challenged the Biblical accounts of the origin of man recorded in the Book of Genesis, preachers arose who—like Henry Ward Beecher— were the popular cultural interpreters to their communities. Finally, in the twentieth century, the impact of psychology and psychoanalysis led to several ministers' specializing in the new diagnostic techniques for the mentally frustrated and disturbed. The twentieth century has brought to full fruition, particularly in the well-to-do urban churches, the idea that the ministry is a combination of specialized techniques of service to the community—preaching, educational, liturgical, and psychological. The community no longer means the members in good standing of a particular church, but the neighborhood which it serves. Other specialized ministries to sections of the community were military, school, and hospital chaplaincies.*

The three novels which have been selected illustrate three developments in the idea of the minister as the community leader. The rural and urban Methodist ministry, where the pastor is also something of a leader of good causes in the area where he ministers, is sympathetically recorded in a novel written by the son of a Methodist parsonage, Hartzell Spence, in *One Foot in Heaven* (1940).† The social service type of ministry as exercised in an institutional church by an Episcopalian

---

* Thomas Wolfe in *The Web and the Rock* (1938) has an admirable account of a sincere and successful college chaplain, George Webber, who as an Episcopalian, is quite unofficially attached to the Southern Baptist College of Pine Rock.

† This work is part fact (true reminiscence) and part fiction, like most novels; in this one, however, there is probably a larger proportion due to the memory than to the imagination.

minister is described by James Gould Cozzens in *Men and Brethren* (1936). The minister as cultural interpreter of the up-to-date in philosophy and aesthetics is wittily satirized, yet with seriousness behind the satire, in *The Mackerel Plaza* (1958) by Peter De Vries.

These types of ministry have, of course, their dangers as well as their advantages. They may confuse the *wants* of the community with its *needs*, which are not always the same. They may be attempting to compete with the secular world which pays its specialists better and has so many more of them available. They may, moreover, corrupt the Gospel in the process, leading men to seek God, not for Himself but for the by-products of Christianity, such as morale, mental health, social contacts; and may enable those who need a radical cure for their egocentricism to rest in superficial ease in Sion. They may turn the minister into an efficient executive of social service committees, or a master of ceremonies for their entertainments, or into a mere budget raiser or culture monger. It is the usefulness of the satirists, like De Vries, that they startle and surprise us out of the conventional rut which the latest and most successful type of ministry may keep us in. The 'latest' is often only a novel expression of this-worldliness. What H. Richard Niebuhr has described as the weakness of the culture-accommodating gospel of the nineteenth-century liberals may equally well apply to the implicit teaching behind the practice of the minister as a community director:

A God without wrath brought men without sin into a kingdom without judgment through the ministrations of a Christ without a cross.[2]

The only satisfactory correction of this tendency is a concern that the Gospel of the Incarnation, the Cross, and the Resurrection shall be preached in the sermons, witnessed to in the liturgy, and its benefits received in the Sacraments, and that the preaching and liturgical ministry shall be the primary concern and fountain from which the communal activities flow, and that dependence upon the Holy Spirit shall be the dynamo and generator of all the practical activities.

1. Hartzell Spence

One Foot in Heaven is a kindly and amusing recounting of his father's life as a Methodist minister by Hartzell Spence, with appreciation of his sterling qualities of courage, integrity, generosity, and ingenuity, and a tolerant eye for his little inconsistencies and peccadilloes. The title is explained by one sentence:

We of his household, balanced, precarious Christians, with one foot in Heaven and one on earth, not daring to plant both feet solidly either way.[3]

Like every minister's son, young Spence cannot forget what it is, in Milton's words, to be 'the cynosure of neighboring eyes' in the goldfish-bowl existence; admirably put forth in James Street's novels by his descriptions of the powerful and often spiteful pressures of the congregation on the minister, and their way of retaliating on him through exposing unconventional conduct on the part of his children. Throughout the book one senses that the author is recalling a time which was happy but also anxious; anxious because of this demand for stilted respectability and anxious also because of financial insecurity.

This leader of his community had to be a most versatile man, a jack of all trades, as his wife had to be a most careful manager. Her duties consisted in feeding and clothing the children, entertaining guests, acting as the buffer between her husband and the congregation and between him and his children, all on a shoestring budget. For himself the essential combination of qualifications needed was almost impossible. As Spence writes:

To be worth his salt, a preacher must be sincerely pious, narrow to the point of bigotry in his private life, a master politician with both his parish and the higher church organization, and a financial juggler just one step up the heavenly ladder from Wall Street. Above all, he must have a quick wit, the courage of a first-century martyr, and a stomach that will not complain of meager rations. If he possesses these qualities and a wife who will neither offend anyone nor outshine her husband, he is eligible for a country parish.[4]

Additional qualifications are needed for a city pulpit, including

an unimpeachable respect for his own ability, the oratorical fire of Savonarola, the organizational genius of a minority politician, and, if possible, a couple of sons studying for the ministry. If, in addition, he is adept at flattery, he may eventually become a bishop.[5]

The early years were marked by poverty. He began at Lake- ton, in northern Iowa, in 1904 with a salary of $385 per annum, *if* this could be collected in full from the circuit. He had to be a practical man for his family could not afford to call in plumbers or painters. Moreover, his church rarely attracted the opulent type, who went to the Congregationalists or the Epis- copalians, nor the scrupulous tithers of the Baptists nor the regularly generous such as supported the Roman Catholic Church. At Fort Dodge, his second charge, he would never ask for a desperately needed item of furniture or furnishing. If a new rug was urgently required in the study the family contrived it so that the steward would trip over an exposed surface. The children's shoes were bought from the marriage fees of country couples who came to the town to be married, but had no con- tacts with a town church. A family conspiracy of father, mother, and son lured the couple to the parsonage: the son was the informant who told the father, wherever he might be visiting, of the marital suspects, while mother, chatting gaily, kept them until father returned.[6] The town clerk, also a Methodist, was in the conspiracy. Yet the minister was not always paid a fee, and the author records a society wedding in a well-to-do Methodist Church for which his father had superintended two rehearsals and donated a handsome wedding gift to the wealthy pair, to receive no acknowledgment of his services.

The minister was an excellent example of the narrow strength of pietism, not without its moments of liberalism, however. He did not only avoid evil, but also the appearance of evil, and he wished his children to do the same. When his son returned from school one afternoon:

'What are you eating, son?' he called out.
'Candy,' I answered, holding up a chocolate cigar.
'Let me see it.' He took the cigar as though it were an evil thing.
'Where did you get this?'
'Down at the corner. Mr. Jansen sells them for a penny, but he gave me this because I didn't have any money.'
Father regarded the chocolate thoughtfully.
'I don't think, son,' he said finally, 'that you ought to have this kind of candy. Chocolate is all right. A little after school is good for you. But I don't like you to be touching anything that looks like tobacco. It might tempt you later to buy a real cigar, and smoking is sinful. I'll just throw this away.'
Tossing the cigar in a wastebasket, he put his hand in his pocket and brought up a penny.
'Here,' he said, 'get something else.'[7]

His ethical code was severely hedged about by the New Testament and the Methodist Book of Discipline. His was a moral world of blacks and whites, with little place for grays, for the latter represented compromises. Yet he was as much concerned about the spirit as the letter of Scripture and of the Christian life, and it would be an utter travesty to suppose that his doctrine and his behavior were merely formal, external, or conventional. Nor was he, like some pietists, singularly prone to uncharitableness and puffed up with an air of superiority or even complacency. His sermons were not literal in their interpretation of the Scripture. As his son waggishly puts it:

He never took literally the admonition from the Sermon on the Mount: If thy right arm cause thee to stumble, cut it off. Father had no desire for a church full of left-handed worshippers. Some of them looked bad enough from the pulpit as it was! [8]

He was, in fact, capable of acts of the most spontaneous generosity, which a conventional and calculating minister would have avoided. He is willing to hold revival services even if the rather stolid and unemotional Presbyterians will benefit most from the converts. He is willing to bury a suicide, when no one else can be found to preside at the interment. He it is who stands at the lonely graveside when the son of a murderer is buried and there is no one else to mourn the boy.[9] He is the one who arranges for a pregnant, unmarried girl to have her baby in a far distant city, places her child in reliable hands, so that no spiteful and bitter tongues may hurt one who has sufficiently injured herself, and gives her a chance of a respected future.

Like every minister worth his salt, he has many problems, and the chief of them is trying to raise the spiritual temperature of a church that relapses so readily into Laodiceanism. The usual nostrum is, of course, to hold revivals, but the Rev. Mr. Spence has his own definite ideas of how to conduct them. (In some of them he is like London Wingo in James Street's *The Gauntlet*.) He greatly disliked two characteristics of the usual revivals: the assessment of the sincerity of the revival by the noise and frequency of the 'Hallelujahs' raised by the old-time 'shouting Methodists,' and the superficiality of the 'change' in the so-called converts. He also disapproved of the appeal to fear caused by dangling sinners over the pit of Hell.

The author gives a very vivid picture of the old-time Methodist revivalist bishop and his technique, which shows how much room there was for improvement:

I remember an elderly Methodist bishop who worked for an hour and a half to thaw out his pre-war congregation. He tried all his tricks but met only stony silence. Exasperated, finally, he interrupted his sermon to ask, 'Are those bald heads I see down there or tombstones?'

Then he would pick on one member of the congregation, ask him if he had a voice, make him use it, until it grew from a whisper to a shout of 'Praise the Lord.' After a long time he got the entire congregation to use their lungs to the full, fairly bawling 'Hallelujah!' The exhausted bishop then mopped his brow and smiled.

'That's better,' he said, 'I was afraid for a moment I was addressing heathen.' [10]

This was definitely not the way to conduct a modern Methodist revival meeting in the opinion of Mr. Spence.

His strategy was worth studying. On the first night he concentrated on his regular congregation. His aim was to bring them to a sense of guilt, of the need for forgiveness and for consecration. He never made the mistake of charging them with Sin, but only with *sins!*

'How many of you,' he asked, leaning across his pulpit intimately, 'have been uncharitable towards a neighbor or have not settled a quarrel? How many of you have neglected their children's religious training because you were too lazy to get up in time for Sunday School? Do you harbor a grudge against a business competitor? Have you overworked your employees or your hired girl? Can you come to the altar of Christ with a pure heart? Or is your soul so crowded with little sins that there is no room for Christ?' [11]

The necessary mood of penitence was created by the quiet chanting of the hymn by the choir, 'Just as I am without one plea. . .' Then followed words of encouragement—the main point of which was that each one wanted to live as Christ desires, but each has sinned, and requires forgiveness. Finally, there followed an act of resolve:

I ask all those who want to follow Christ to join me here at the altar. Let God and your neighbours know that you humbly repent your sins and that you earnestly desire to live the Christian life. Come! [12]

In the end they came, as he told anecdotes to remove their lingering doubts. Thus, having persuaded the regular congregation to renew their vows to God, he had a nucleus of an inspirational group that filtered through the audience in the course of the succeeding meetings.

At one such revival there were 675 cards signed, including 103 strangers with no church affiliation. The gain to the Methodists was slight, a mere eleven members. When Mrs. Spence wondered why so many converts were going over to the Presbyterians, and so few to the Methodists, the rueful minister brought his humor to the rescue and replied,

The Methodists, mother, are building a new church. You can't expect a sinner to mend his ways and sign a building pledge in the same year.[13]

This minister, also, like London Wingo, has to combine the wisdom of the serpent with the innocence of the dove to get his plans accomplished in the Church. It is evidenced in the way he persuaded reluctant stewards to agree to the building of a new church out in the suburbs: when he has convinced them that the present church building can be sold advantageously, that another temporary building can be hired cheaply, and that they will get a profitable return for the money they lay out.

The same shrewdness is exhibited in the spiritual blackmail he has to employ against the woman who had spread the story that his son had compromised a young girl in the town.

It seems that he is stubborn in the defense of his convictions, and it is only the influence of his wife that can make him interpret the Biblical injunctions liberally. There is a most amusing incident when she has to argue her husband into a very liberal interpretation of Sabbatarianism to permit the family to go driving in their new car on a Sunday. Mother's specious arguments, which finally prevail, are three. There is no veto against car driving in the Book of Discipline (how could there be, since cars were not thought of when it was drawn up?). The gasoline can be put in the tank on Saturday, thus requiring no extra human assistance on Sunday. Finally, she argues that the new machine may be used to convey people to church on Sunday who would otherwise be unable to attend because of infirmity or distance. The ironic sequel is that the family does, indeed, go for its long drive only to run out of fuel, and they finally have to be accommodated at a farmer's house. It will have become clear already that this book is also a tribute to the tact and astonishing industry of the minister's wife. Her gifts to charity made from so exiguous a salary as her husband's were marvels of planning and saving, as was her ready hospitality.

His gifts as a community director were given the greatest scope when Mr. Spence was called to minister to Morningside Church in Sioux City. Here he had a congregation of professional men, academics, and their families and pupils. It was also a time to try the souls of men, for Britain was at war with Germany and the United States was expected to follow suit in due time. He was soon concerned with Red Cross, Liberty Loan, and War Savings Stamp drives. Army barracks were constructed on the college campus. When they were completed he introduced himself to the major, who was commandant of the cantonment, saying that he'd 'like a job as chaplain to this outfit.' He made it a point to know every one of the lads personally. His was not now a ministry of conversion, but of compassion. This is significantly the mark of a ministry of community leadership in the modern world. In two weeks he knew everybody by his full name, but not once did he try to convert the lads or exhort them to make their peace with God lest they be killed in battle. Instead, he helped them to write letters home, straightened out their thinking on problems of calculus and chemistry, and wrote their English essays. He was a companion and hoped his example would lead them to respect his way of life.[14] His only failures, for a time, were a group of a dozen newcomers who had no respect for him at all. They refused his invitations to the parsonage, and when he joined their baseball game they stopped playing. One day he saw them playing a gambling game. The rest of the story must be told in the novelist's words:

One day he came upon six of them shooting craps. He stood by them until he saw how the game was played, then sat down among them. They were expecting a moral lecture. To head it off, one lad defiantly tossed him the dice.
'Try it, Parson, it will do you good.'
Father calmly took the dice, blew on them, and shook them.
The boys were surprised; their idea of a chaplain was a stiff-backed soul-saver.

One of them bet that he wouldn't turn up winning numbers. To everyone's unconcealed amazement, he did. His opponent exclaimed,

'Well, I'll be damned!'
The chaplain did not then wish to reform, but only to be accepted, so he said, 'That is Hell, isn't it?'
One of the stunned boys recovered sufficiently to call,
'Say, chaplain, you forgot your winnings.'[15]

He called back that he couldn't accept it, as he had no money in his pocket to pay had he lost. From that time on he was chaplain to them all in fact as well as in name. If 'guts' are what an army chaplain needs, Spence had an abdomen-full! In time the men became less fond of card games as their chaplain introduced bowling, curling, and even cricket to prepare them to meet the British when they were sent overseas. He proved himself able to be, with the apostle Paul, 'all things to all men'! His wider ministry of compassion was a success.

This is not a great novel, not even a serious one. The faithful and generally undramatic ministry it describes neither scales the Alps of heroic witness nor plumbs the marshes and quicksands of despair. But it is an accurate and warm-hearted account of the many difficulties and irritations of the ministry and of its smaller triumphs. The constant friction of petty irritations can also be extremely exhausting: difficulties with ancient choir members who will not be removed, malicious gossip, pettifogging criticism of the minister's children, the ruthless competitiveness of the women in their church clothes and in the pies they bake for church suppers, the sheer obduracy of the human heart. It is also a documentary of the dreams of the minister—which have almost always to be cut to practical size to fit the half-hearted enthusiasms of the people—and of the hopes of marriage and the pathos of bereavement. There are recorded here no gigantic struggles between faith and unbelief; but there is a shrewd dialectical contest between Spence and Horrigan, the agnostic dentist, in which the minister scores most of the debating points, and gets his adversary to admit at least that the morality of Western civilization is Christian and that Jesus was its founder; also that while he, Horrigan, accepts the Christian code those who hold the Christian faith have a greater incentive and a larger consolation than those who try to heed the Christian imperatives outside the Church. Here there are no great heroisms, but, perhaps, something very much more difficult—and that is the faithful, uncomplaining, steady, courageous, and cheerful service of God, evoked by a sincere and sacrificial love of Him; its reward for the minister is the ungrudging admiration of the community in which he works, and it goes far beyond the confines of his church or indeed of all the churches in the town.

2. James Gould Cozzens

In James Gould Cozzens' Men and Brethren (1936) we have what may well be considered the finest study in the English language of the Protestant minister in the twentieth century. Cozzens seems to have made it his considered plan to study each of the professions in turn, with consummate care, attention to detail, and subtle imaginative identification. The medical man is the center of chief interest in The Last Adam (1933), the lawyer in The Just and the Unjust (1942), and the military man in Guard of Honor (1948). In the same way Men and Brethren is a remarkably percipient study of an intelligent, cultured, and compassionate clergyman, a moderate Episcopalian who is the Vicar of St. Ambrose's Chapel, an institutional and settlement type of church on the East side of New York City.

What first impresses us is the variety of clerical portraits with which the author presents us. The dominating character is, of course, Ernest Cudlipp, the Vicar, who is in his middle forties and is the director of a considerable religious and social community, with its Parish House, offering recreational facilities for youth, its Dispensary which has two doctors attached to it and some social welfare workers. The center of this community is the Vicarage which, apart from housing the celibate Vicar and his two assistant clergy, seems to be a temporary home for intellectual or Bohemian waifs and strays linked by need and friendship to the Vicar himself. It is in the setting of the Vicarage that we chiefly encounter Ernest Cudlipp, where any semblance of an ordered life is interrupted by the constant knocking at the door or by the insistent telephone, his links with the world of need.

The other clergy introduced in the novel are an interesting group. There is the aged and rheumy missionary returned from Alaska, Mr. Johnston, a tired but indefatigable visitor in the neighborhood of the small, seedy tenements, elevated trains, and dismal backyards. He is superficially a most unprepossessing character, perpetually apologizing for himself, with his half-finished sentences and constant self-depreciation. He is poor, shabby, has no affectations, and inclines to a sentimental turn in the choice of hymns. Yet he is a man without guile, and in the second section of the book he comes into his own at the death-bed of Mrs. Hawley.

And Johnston's few possessions, in their basic simplicity, speak of great humility and untroubled faith and consideration of others. He has only two photographs in his bedroom: one of the Bishop of Alaska and the other shows a group of Alaskans or Indians gathered below a low shack on which a cross stands, and the background of barrenness and freezing cold tells its own story of missionary endurance. On the desk are two volumes: The Bible and *The Imitation of Christ*. Cudlipp reflects as he looks at the exhausted old man on his bed, and sees his few belongings:

The rewards of his hard, bare, devoted life, the unsearchable riches of Christ, were given him in the perfect freedom and perfect joy of needing nothing.[16]

Johnston has an entry where the more subtle and cultured Cudlipp is perplexed. What can match the sincere simplicity with

which he tries to bring the dying woman back to serious concern for her soul? His words were:

Jesus is near. He knows. He hears. Won't you speak to Him?[17]

Cudlipp's other assistant priest is an ordained graduate student
from General Theological Seminary, who helps him during the
summer months. He is buoyantly optimistic, a man of sound,
if not subtle, mind in a magnificently healthy body. For him
there are no aggravating doubts, only certainties. His syncre-
tistical enthusiasms combine some unlikely companions: Christian Socialism, the Oxford Group Movement, and the theology
of Karl Barth. His one moderately urgent problem is one of
morals not of faith: shall he marry or not?

Cudlipp's superior, the Rector of the mother church of Holy
Innocents' with its two million dollar endowment, of which St.
Ambrose's Chapel is the poor relation, is admirably sketched.
Dr. Lamb's eighteenth-century patrician profile, with its frosty
blue eyes, aquiline nose, silvered hair, and expensively cut
clothes, has the right glacial effect. He seems just the man to
keep the affluent and influential Vestry of Holy Innocents' in
its proper place. But he is, in fact, a man whose amiability and
courtesy are real, but his charitableness is never allowed to
break the conventions. It is significant that the two occasions
on which he has to express his concern over Cudlipp's attitudes
are ones in which expediency in him is opposed to a charity in
Cudlipp which is unconcerned about public opinion. On the
first occasion, Cudlipp has invited a Jewish Rabbi to preach in
the Chapel and Lamb, while saying that he is in sympathy with
Cudlipp, and even deploring the Bishop of the diocese as a bigot,
yet wishes Cudlipp to withdraw the invitation so as not to incur
the Bishop's displeasure further. On the second and more serious
occasion, he demands that Cudlipp send from the Vicarage a

former High Anglican monk who is a homosexual, again solely for reasons of expediency.

The local Roman Catholic priest is merely a telephone introduction. But it is enough to convey the author's dislike of that vast organization which the priest represents. Father Maloney, whom Cudlipp is persuading to come to Mrs. Hawley's deathbed once he has discovered she was born and brought up a Catholic, seems reluctant to come to the woman, and agrees only when Cudlipp says he will have no other alternative but to telephone the Dominicans to send one of their fathers along. Rome is, for Cozzens, the home of dogmatic authoritarianism, of the vulgar sweating masses, of the tawdry art of liturgical aids. Some suggestion of this is given in his description of Father Maloney.

Ernest saw his pale, solid face, moony and luminous; the soft full neck, one single slanting line from the point of his chin to the edge of his collar. In the least cough or throat-clearing sounded the unique, peculiar air of authority and condescension; the bureaucratic, to Ernest not very agreeable, everyday voice of Rome, which went so naturally with the power of the keys.[18]

Already, then, the novel has introduced the subtle, cultured, and courageously compassionate hero as one type of parson; and, in addition, there is the expedient Rector, the self-effacing simpleton of Christ (Johnston), the cheerful and vigorous young assistant, Quinn, the bureaucratic priest, Maloney, and the highly dramatic homosexual High Anglican monk. It is a fair account of the variety of personalities in the ministry.

The plot has been concentrated so as to show what goes on in the mind of an Episcopalian minister within a period of twenty-four hours. For this purpose Cozzens has to employ the techniques that will render an extension of time and the contrast of situations credible and yet keep the concentration. This is deftly done by the backtracking of the memory, by associational links, photographs, a church annual report, and the rumination of his hero. At the same time the impression of the interruptions made in the plans of the minister by these constant calls on the telephone or knocks on the door for help from demanding people, of his being utterly at the beck and call of the needy, the sick, the perplexed, and the desperate, is admirably conveyed. The novel is, indeed, a tribute to the devotion and exhaustion of the modern ministry. Cudlipp is truly a 'Man' among his 'Brethren.'

It is also an interesting glimpse into the contacts that an Episcopalian city minister makes in his calling. It is, one may guess, a defect in the novel that so many of the persons who call upon the Rev. Ernest Cudlipp's services belong to the same social milieu: a former actress who is having marital trouble; a poet who has seduced a married woman who was educated at Vassar; a painter's widow who is—like the Vassar woman—intending to commit suicide; this is the group he knows most intimately. The juvenile delinquents, of whom there must have been several in his parish, do not appear in the foreground of attention except one, Jimmy, and he is disposed of *in absentia*. One suspects that the part-time director of music who sells neckties for a living is only tolerated because he likes plain song and is an amateur composer. In short, the Vicar's advice is sought almost exclusively among the Bohemian coterie and on the subject of love. He is, too much, 'By Love Possessed.' The only exception is the dying Mrs. Hawley, who is a member of the lower-middle class, and here, it seems, that the humble, aged Johnston is of more use than the Vicar can be. This narrowing of the community, especially in a downtown church, seems extremely unlikely in real life and may arise from the apparent inability of Cozzens to make poor or unprofessional people interesting. Certainly, his lower-income bracket characters are stereotypes. Lily, the Negro maid, is only a grumpy, plump, and necessary

evil, not a person. The elevator boy is merely a type of prying
sneak. Critics have called Cozzens a snob; it may merely be that
his intellectual and aesthetic interests have prevented him from
seeing what is the privilege of every sensitive minister, and Cudlipp was certainly that, namely, the personalities of the under-
privileged.[19] The note of charity is conspicuously present in the
portrait of Cudlipp, but the note of comprehensiveness, in a
word, of catholicity, is as obviously lacking.

Cudlipp appears as a fine human personality, with many sides.
He is conspicuously a man of aesthetic taste. A connoisseur of
ecclesiastical architecture of many styles (who prefers the
genuine Colonial to the neo-Gothic fake), one who can cite
poetry (from Marvell to the moderns), and who knows how to
order the appropriate wine. He is also a man of intellectual ability and great psychological insight, who can readily penetrate
the false romanticism with which people mask their least cred-
itable appetites. A person of great sensitivity, he knows exactly
when to be sympathetic and when to be firm. He holds his
eminently sensible views with clarity and conviction, but without undue dogmatism. His pre-eminent gift, however, is sheer
compassion. He never refuses a call, is never perfunctory in lis-
tening to the troubles of others, and frequently risks his reputation as a celibate in order to stand by wronged women, without
letting sentiment interfere with his diagnosis as a soul surgeon. In
fact, it is probably because of his celibacy that so many women
turn to him for help, because he is not soiled with the lust of most
of their male acquaintances, yet is a virile enough human being
of charm and consideration. The oncoming of middle age has
made him much less interested in speculative theology, though if
he had time he would wish to hunt for the experience that lay
behind Calvin's pitiless logic in *The Institutes*. He is perceptive
in discovering the apparent reason for his young colleague's ad-
diction to the Barthian theology: he is provided with a weapon

with which to beat his communistic friends; and when they point out the irrationality of some of the Christian doctrines, he is able to reply that the revelation of the Word of God transcends the limitations of human rationality. With all this, Cudlipp is yet perfectly honest with himself, and does not paint the shadow even of a halo of complacency on his self-portrait. His creed is always charity before expediency. Yet it would be unfair to label him as merely the product of the Social Gospel, for he believes in the primacy of the spiritual world and of the culture and discipline of the spiritual life. Even if he is critical of much pietism, a hint, no more, of his cosmic and incarnational theology is given in his refutation of it. To the worldly Alice's shocked 'What would Jesus say?' he has the reply:

You mustn't drag Our Lord into everything. It's a low evangelical form of anthropomorphism. Instead, try wondering what the lightning coming out of the east, or what the Incarnate Logos would say.[20]

Here, again, Cozzens might have made the theological basis of his minister's vocation much clearer if he had allowed us to see him preparing a sermon, or discussing with a searching skeptic. Furthermore, in the hurry-scurry of his life, we are not allowed one glimpse of Cudlipp in the sanctuary, reading the Prayer-Book or using some other form of spiritual discipline. It is not enough to imply, by the casual use of the name of St. John of the Cross in a heated discussion with a renegade priest, that Cudlipp is an adept at the devotional life. Doctrine and devotion normally play in the life of an Episcopal minister a most impressive role, and they curiously do not in Cudlipp's life. The Sacraments seem not to exist.

Cudlipp's ministry, according to the novel, is best realized in directing the tasks of his subordinates in the group pastorate, and in the tenderness and firmness with which he counsels the defeated and the desperate. An excellent example of his technique in giving counsel, with its combination of sympathy, firmness, and practical steps, is his dealing with Geraldine Binney, who has been having, although she is a married woman, an affair with a young poet, who has grown tired of her. She is two months pregnant and is on the verge of suicide. As Cudlipp enters her hotel apartment, his first words are:

Don't ever think of doing that, Geraldine. Besides being cheap and silly, it wouldn't be forgiven you, either in this world or the next. There are too many people involved. How do you think they'd feel? [21]

His next duty is to prevent her romanticizing herself as a tragic heroine, to let her see that her so-called love affair is only a cheap and sullied self-indulgence. At the same time he must counter despair with hope and a new sense of responsibility. He reminds her of her three children. He tells her that the poet is having another affair. The practical man arranges for her to have an interview with a woman doctor the next day. Finally, he insists that she kneel to receive absolution, that she may realize that God will forgive her even if it will be years before she forgives herself. As a symbol of his belief that she is once again in control of herself, he gives her a tablet of the veronal which she had proposed—by an overdose—to use as the instrument of suicide. In this desperate situation he is essentially at his best. He is very like Paton's Anglican priest, Father Vincent.

Cudlipp is a man of remarkable honesty, as well as compassion. He has no illusions about himself. As he contemplates the vast new Byzantine edifice of Holy Innocents', rebuilt to celebrate the hundredth anniversary of the foundation of the parish, he notices that the Collect for the festival of the Holy Innocents' day has been inscribed on the marble of the entablature, and that it ascribes to God, what is to him the repugnant sentiment, 'who . . . madest infants to glorify Thee by their death.' He comments,

As rector of a parish like this I wouldn't last a year; . . . The truth is I have no tact. It isn't that I wouldn't stand for it; it's that I couldn't. I don't know how.[22]

He is a man of intellectual and moral integrity, and because of his refusal to make compromises, he will never attain to success in the higher ranks of the clergy. Yet, such is his modesty, he interprets this characteristic as a flaw in self-control.

He does not wear his faith on his sleeve, because he knows how shallow are the emotional exhibitionists, how complacent are the narrow pietists. In the conclusion of the book, he gives a very rational, and entirely unflattering account of how he came to choose his vocation. Yet in this very reasonable account of his calling, there are overtones of a sense of the Divine election and providential ordering of the world. His very ordinary account includes the matter-of-fact enumeration of factors: he had the right temperament; he found that he could make people obey him; a priest he admired influenced him; the overspending of his father made it necessary for him to join a church choir to earn pocket money and this led to his becoming a member of the Acolytes' Guild.

In short, the Church gave me an opening. I saw it.

This hardly seems an adequate explanation to Geraldine Binney, who says, bemusedly:

'You mean, it just happened?'
'Can you conceive of that?' he asked.
'A year ago could you have dreamed where you would be today? A year ago, was there one chance in a million that I would ever exchange a word with you. Only in God's omniscience. Here you are. Here am I.'
She continued to look at him.
'You do mean, then,' she said, 'that really you believe God meant you to be a priest?'
'Just as He means everything to be, that is.'[23]

As the book ends, he is reading to the recuperating woman the parable of the talents, which is the authority and explanation of his vocation.

There is only one flaw in the character of Cudlipp, and this, one suspects, is the fault of his portrayer, and it is, as has been suggested, an unlikely failing in the vicar of a downtown parish. It is a curious insensitivity to the common man, which occasionally reveals that his fastidiousness is snobbishness. It is reminiscent of Maugham's Vicar of Blackstable and his contempt for Dissenting ministers, as when in utter disdain Cudlipp refers witheringly to the Roman Catholic priest, Father Maloney, as 'that common little Mick.' There was a suggestion of it earlier in the reference to the 'monkey-face' of Lily, Cudlipp's Negro maid, and in an anti-Semitic reference to one of the Vestrymen who had been converted to Christianity. This is, I suspect, the fault of the limited imagination of the author, because the characteristic reappears in *By Love Possessed.*

This novel, despite its defects, is an extremely sensitive portrayal of a modern Protestant minister and that is a great rarity in contemporary fiction. It is adept in its discussion of the themes that might be expected to engage the interest of an Episcopalian priest: the advantages of celibacy; if it is advisable to tell a patient that she is dying; the contemporary theological fashions (Barthianism, the Oxford Group, Christian Social Action, and even the blessed word 'ecumenical' is deftly introduced); the embarrassment of a settlement church depending upon the income endowed by robber barons; the problems and finer points of ecclesiastical architecture and music. Its conversations are taut and never a word is wasted, and the style is freighted with Shakespearian and Biblical references, and is rarely as self-consciously tortuous as in *By Love Possessed;* there is subtlety in the vocabulary, and occasionally wit. But, above all, there is a profound understanding of the ministry as an exhausting, al-

ways interrupted, intelligent, and compassionate treating of
mankind as the brethren of Christ and, in this novel of the
group ministry, a deep sense of caring for the whole personality
by cutting away deceptive illusions through skillful soul
surgery, by warm hospitality, by sensible and practical arrangements, by an unwearying charity, resembling that of the Good
Samaritan, that extends to body as well as to soul.

A final question remains to be asked and answered: How
adequate is Cozzens' understanding of the Christian faith? It
has been observed that Ernest Cudlipp is not interested at all
in speculative theology, it seems that morality and compassion
are his basic concerns. It was further observed that the devotional life is of peripheral concern, and the sacramental life of
none in his vocation. His understanding of compassion is limited
by his fastidious dislike of vulgarity and vulgar people. One is
bound, therefore, to ask: Does religion mean anything more
than decent morality for James Gould Cozzens? It seems hard
to avoid that conclusion, since his attack against the Catholic
Church, more thoroughly developed in *By Love Possessed*, is
not only an attack against authoritarianism as an abdication of
the freedom of the intelligent man but also, by implication, a
denial of the possibility of supernatural revelation. His strong
preference for moderate Episcopalianism is very significant, for
he dislikes the ardors of the left-wing and the obedience required by the right-wing denominations. What he seems to desire is a respect for tradition, good manners, sensitivity in human
relationships, an appreciation for culture and aesthetics—and
this is humanism! It is very significant that in *By Love Possessed*
Arthur Winner agrees to become Senior Warden of Christ
Church largely because this is what his father had been before
him. He reflects on what that soundly rational man, had thought
of the Church, and its teachings:

The stuff of this myth had long been the sacred fiction of the Man of Reason's people, his race. A fable so venerated, around which their civilization, for century on century, had formed itself, had a vested right. Were such established usages of piety to be lightly scouted? 24

Cozzens' own philosophy seems to be Stoicism without heroics, facing life's inevitable tragedies with dignity, and, until they come, performing one's vocation with the utmost conscientiousness. For him, then, religion can only be construed as crutches and blinkers for the weak. That passion certainly blinds the reason, he neither attributes to original sin, nor believes it to be cured by grace. Religion helps others, and he respects their rather absurd but traditional convictions provided they are accompanied with compassion and a respect for culture; but religion cannot help him. Ultimately, then, the missing dimensions in *Men and Brethren*, in his portrayal of his Episcopalian minister, are theological, and he presents us with the 'Social Gospel' without the fullness of the Gospel that is its justification and motivation; as in *By Love Possessed* he presents every variety of love, tender or grasping, except the sheer generosity of sacrificial Christian love.

3. Peter De Vries

The Mackerel Plaza (1958) is a scintillating satire on the life of the most modernist of modern ministers, yet it would be a mistake to dismiss the whole novel as a *jeu d'esprit*. Kingsley Amis has said that De Vries is the most serious comic writer on either side of the Atlantic and Amis himself writes his comic novels with as serious a purpose as Dickens. The hero, Mr. Mackerel, is minister of the People's Liberal Church in a commuters' town in Connecticut. He has problems enough with the living, but his chief problem is a ghost—the utterly undeserved respect in which his congregation holds his dead wife, whom they wish to honor by building a central Mackerel Plaza.

Mackerel's characteristics are quickly divulged. He is an aesthete, first and foremost. Indeed, the novel opens with his complaint to the municipal Zoning Board about a revivalist sign in orange and green phosphorescent paint with the vulgar legend 'Jesus Saves.' It worries him so much that he cannot study. The secretary whom he contacts by telephone to make his complaint thinks that he is worried about a possible fall in property values. He indignantly replies:

Oh! property values! Please get that out of your head, miss. Do you think I own the parsonage I live in? I'm talking about spiritual values. Spiritual and aesthetic ones. How do you expect me to write a sermon with that thing staring me in the face? How do you expect me to turn out anything fit for civilized consumption? [25]

Culture comes a close second to aesthetics in the Mackerel's rather spotty scale of values. When the secretary asks him, 'What does the Apostle Paul say?' he rapidly dismisses the question as irrelevant.

I have no idea, but Oscar Wilde reminds us that while crime is not vulgar, vulgarity is a crime. Jesus doesn't save any of these people [orthodox pietists], because all they want to do is boost their paltry souls into heaven, while completely shirking the obligation to *evolve*. What we see around us is not a revival at all but a kind of backsliding, and I do mean that—a failure of taste as *well* as nerve.

He concludes his telephonic rehearsal of his last week's sermon with the words:

Let us graft onto the Christian principle of selflessness, as Auden so cogently urges, the Freudian one of maturity, and come up with an ideal suited to our era. [26]

His creed is, otherwise, largely a series of haughty negations of what the vulgar masses and the long Christian centuries have believed.

As might be expected, Mackerel wants to be thought anything but a minister. He finally visits the Zoning Board office to make his complaint in person. The well-rounded secretary's reaction and even more his own are interesting.

'Oh, *you're* the—?' She recoiled a step in surprise, then laughed and said apologetically,
'But you're young. You can't be more than thirty-five. And you certainly don't look like a preacher.'

De Vries comments on Mackerel's response:

This pleased Mackerel. Mackerel so disliked the term preacher, and so abhorred the term brother, as designations for the clergy that he was always grateful for their inapplicability to himself. It was not merely the wish to elude prototype that lay at the bottom of this, though this wish did exist in Mackerel to an exquisite degree; it was, more cardinally, a fear of quarantine, a desire to belong to his species—in which the deferential 'Reverend' tended to blur one's membership—that made him want ever so much to be known simply as Mister Mackerel.[27]

For most ministers the most insidious temptation they ever face is the wish to run with the Hound of Heaven and the socialite and intellectual hares of earth. For Mackerel it was no temptation, for he did not believe that the Hound of Heaven was more than an outmoded and unsuitable metaphor for an illusion. The hares of culture (more often the pomaded poodles of pretentiousness) he found quite irresistible.

If traditional theology was taboo, even an emasculated theism was unacceptable, for it was the anthropomorphism acceptable only to the mooning adolescents who put coins in juke-boxes to listen to the saccharine religious ballads of the Hit Parade.

Whenever he cites a text, it is merely a pretext for ingenious heterodoxy. The Saviour of orthodox Christianity is reduced to the level of a decent first-century Oscar Wilde, with a wit like a razor, a master of riposte and epigram, and an obvious neurotic. In fact, Mackerel fancies himself as an improver of the Sermon on the Mount. He revised one of the Beatitudes as a safety slogan for road-hogs: 'Blessed are the pacemakers for they shall see God.' The gullible and credulous mediocrities who attend any church but his own are, not 'babes and sucklings,' but boobs and suckers.

He will not only revise theology, but liturgy also so that a service is no longer the worship of God but the celebration of the spirit of community interdependence. On one occasion he devised a ritual for a service in a time of community crisis, after the flash-floods had left many families in Connecticut homeless and foodless. He was surprised at the alacrity with which his congregation entered into the spirit of the thing.

Offerings were to be laid on a table below the pulpit this morning in a kind of family processional just before the sermon. During the choir number my eye ranged round the audience, and I must say I was a bit taken aback by the foodstuffs some of the better-heeled commuting members of my flock were clutching: vichyssoise, artichoke hearts, smoked clams, even trout *pâté* were visible among the more standard and more rational donations of canned beans and peas, and peaches and pears. Cocktail snacks for flood victims. One could not restrain the image of groups partaking of these essentials on the roofs of floating homes, nor repress an affectionate smile for the exurbanite givers in their pews. . .

The incorrigible Mackerel then prayed,

Let us hope . . . that a kind Providence will put a speedy end to the acts of God under which we have been laboring.[28]

As might be guessed, Mackerel, denying the existence of a personal God, has a profound dislike of prayers of confession or supplication. Confession, to his fastidious mind, is essentially a private matter, not an opportunity for the emotionally luxuriating to re-enact their scarlet sins. Mackerel refuses prayers of supplication because they offend against his scientific conscience. This is the reason why he will not join the other ministers of Avalon in a communal prayer meeting for rain, which was more than amply answered by the catastrophic floods. This incident Mackerel wittily referred to as merely 'Jehovah's wetness'!

Never has the Christian irrelevance of a community church been more deliciously criticized than in the irony of Mackerel's guided tour of his plant, in which the sanctuary occupies the smallest part of the buildings.

Our church is, I believe, the first split-level church in America. It has five rooms and two baths downstairs—dining area, kitchen and three parlors for committee and group meetings—with a crawl space behind the furnace ending in the hillside into which the structure is built. Upstairs is one huge all-purpose interior, divisible into different-sized compartments by means of sliding-walls and convertible into an auditorium for putting on plays, a gymnasium for athletics and a ball-room for dances.

One observes that Mackerel has not mentioned as yet any feature of the building that has a distinctively religious purpose. The author's ridicule of the up-to-dateness and the uncertainties of liberal and social Christianity, is superbly conveyed in the irony of the following passage:

There is a small worship area at one end. This has a platform cantilevered on both sides, with a free-form pulpit designed by Noguchi. It consists of a slab of marble set on four legs of four delicately differing fruitwoods, to symbolize the Four Gospels, and their failure to harmonize. Behind it dangles a large multi-colored mobile, its interdenominational parts swaying, as one might fancy, in perpetual reminder of the Pauline stricture against 'those blown by every wind of doctrine.' Its proximity to the pulpit inspires a steady flow of more familiar congregational whim, at which we shall not long demur, going on with our tour to say that in back of this building is a newly erected clinic, with medical and neuro-psychiatric wings, both indefinitely expandable. Thus the People's Liberal is a church designed to meet the needs of today, and to serve the whole man. This includes the worship of a God free of outmoded theological definitions and palatable to a mind come of age in the era of Relativity.[29]

Was relativism in the pulpit ever so delightfully castigated? No wonder Mackerel is called the Hemingway of the pulpit for his taut, realistic, ten-minute sermons!

De Vries is also rightly critical of the mediocre standards of the community church's much vaunted dramas. When Mackerel's moral frailties—a consequence of following the gospel according to Havelock Ellis too literally—are about to expose him as the charlatan he is, he considers another church as a sphere of labor in Connecticut. The problem of stage management there does not distress him because the standards of achievement are so low:

I would be expected to handle the dramatics myself, but they would consist in little more than sewing members of the congregation up in sheets and shoving them onstage to yell, Barabbas! Barabbas! Release unto us Barabbas! [30]

The author is perceptive in his implied critique of the sheer subjectivism that underlies Mackerel's eccentric creed, its disguised humanism. To Miss Calico's insistent demand as to the nature of his beliefs, he answers:

I believe in belief. I believe that some binding ethic and some informing myth are necessary to any culture, the myth being to the morality what the wooden forms are to the concrete that is poured into them. When the concrete is hard you can remove the forms (or they will rot away) and the walls will stand of their own.[31]

This is the view that Somerset Maugham's Athelny (in *Of Human Bondage*) had conceived, but it is founded upon a double flaw. In the first place, a morality known to be based upon a myth ceases to have any authority. Secondly, a morality unbased upon a theology or a convincing philosophy lacks the concreteness and the inspiration to better conduct. Mackerel's further declaration that 'faith is a set of demands, not a string of benefits, that a man is under some obligation to better himself, not sit around as he is and wait for Jesus to save him' shows that he is under a double misapprehension: he is too facile about the capacities of human nature unaided by Grace, and he forgets that man can co-operate with Grace in his own salvation, if only by way of preparation.

The sorry reasons why Mackerel entered the ministry are unredeemed by any sense of the providential ordering of God which gave Cozzens' Cudlipp the final justification for his sacred vocation. Mackerel's reasons are nakedly lily-livered.

I became a minister because my mother wanted me to. She made me promise on her deathbed that I would go to divinity school and become a clergyman. I promised her because there was nothing else to do in the circumstances.

His mother was a Dutch Calvinist and he was brought up in Chicago in a hermetically sealed community remote from general American life. He was excited by the fissile tendencies in the Dutch, of whom it is said: 'One Dutchman a Christian; two Dutchmen a congregation; three Dutchmen a heresy.' His father believed in the total depravity of man. Here it is possible that De Vries, behind the mask of satire, is being autobiographical, and that he is theologically lost in the barren No-God's-land which lies between the humanism of Unitarianism and the pitiless logic of the older Calvinistic orthodoxy. It may be significant that De Vries was educated in an institution that was renowned as the stronghold of fundamentalism, Calvin College, Grand Rapids, Michigan.

What is more certain, however, is that he is disgusted alike by vulgar evangelicalism and by a conceited ultra-liberalism. The former is amusingly described in its most obnoxious button-holing form. The rather impertinent approach of the street-corner evangelist, who asks Mackerel, 'Brother have you found Christ?' is answered in Mackerel's best facetious manner: 'Is he lost again?' Yet even behind the religion of incantation: 'Jesus is the power-house! Are you plugged in? Jesus is the transformer! Are you wired up? Jesus is the cable carrying that current from God Almighty! Is your trolley on?'—despite its banality—there is an S.O.S., a poignant cry of need, however stereotyped its expression; behind Mackerel's preaching there seems to be only the need for a neurotic and exotic self-expression.

Yet, even while De Vries satirizes the culture-accommodating characteristic that is central to liberalism in religion, he is also aware of its appeal not only to the snobbish, the cultivated, the aesthetes, and the rootless commuters whose homes are only cocktail bars and dormitories, but for those genuinely concerned to combine religion and reason. Even in Mackerel the poseur, the truth breaks out in the confession and query:

When I was young, a student I mean, we used to debate whether Christ was the son of God. Now the question is whether God is the Father of Christ.[32]

It is with this central question that the smiles of the humorist turn into the furrows of the thinker, Peter De Vries.

Deliberately exaggerated and fantastic as this extravaganza

is meant to be, De Vries is asking some fundamental questions of the Christianity implicit in the community church, and explicit in the most radical reformulations of left-wing theology today. Are these communities merely cells of the self-congratulating exurbanites, or the brotherhood that transcends race and class in Christ? Are their ministers anything more than popular culture-purveyors or directors of physical and mental ambulance work? Do these ten-minute disquisitions on Havelock Ellis and Sigmund Freud, on self-expression and adaptation to the modern folkways, represent the mercy and judgment of the Christian Gospel, or are they merely a little dishonest humanism? Is it fundamentally true that 'Religion is an umbrella that protects us from the rain' and 'Art a parasol with which we shield ourselves from the sun'? De Vries may not be asking these questions directly, but the Christian minister and layman of today must have a direct and convincing answer to these very questions. Moreover, it must be an answer that relates the historic Gospel of the grace of God (and no modernistic ethical culture) to the many-sided needs of the modern Man-in-community, providing the impetus to and the dynamic for Christian living, in the incarnate Christ who is also everyman's contemporary.

VII

The Religious Novel:
A Study in Clerical Gray

Now that the clerical characters of fifteen representative novelists have been considered in detail, it is appropriate to raise two fundamental questions by way of a critique. The first is: What is good religious fiction and how can it be distinguished from sentimental hagiography on the one hand and from mere secular caricature on the other? The second question is: What are the criteria for failure and success in the Christian ministry, and how adequately have the novelists depicted them? Have they been true, in other words, both to the grandeur and squalor of the ministry and priesthood, recalling both the grace of God and the sin of men, the treasure of the Gospel and earthen vessel in which it is contained?

I

Though we have been concerned exclusively with novels delineating clerical characters, it is not in the least necessary for a novel to include a portrait of a minister or priest to be a good religious novel.* It is, however, essential that the domi-

* I am aware that these novels under consideration were not necessarily published as religious novels, and that because of this fact their authors might object to a theological criticism of them. On the other hand, I am merely claiming the Christian's right to evaluate any novel on theological as well as artistic grounds. Moreover, if the novelist includes a religious character he must expect a religious evaluation of that character, if not of the novel as a whole.

nating character be motivated by religious impulses and judged by religious norms. If, however, this is done ostentatiously and crudely, and the character is presented fully armed and wholly sanctified from the start, then we have religious propaganda not literary art, hagiography not biography. We may note that Graham Greene's *The Power and the Glory* is a conscious attempt to provide an alternative to the plaster saint of Catholic hagiography, in which the earthiness of the dissolute and drunken priest who is yet faithful unto death makes him the more obviously the channel of grace, for fidelity is not within his own power. The artistic danger of customary hagiography is the sentimentality which masks the genuine struggle between grace and sin that makes every man an interior civil war, and the prevention of any delineation of development in character. The religious peril of haloed writing is twofold: it makes sainthood incredible and it promotes that Pelagianism which gives the credit for achievement to the hero, not to the hero's God. In fact, however, the very category 'hero' is appropriate only to a humanistic novel; in a religious novel the category 'saint' or 'martyr' is more appropriate since the character is what he is by the empowering of the *sanctifying* Spirit, or as a *witness* to a grace that calls and sustains him. For this reason it was felt that Cronin's Father Francis Chisholm in *The Keys of the Kingdom*, admirable as were his charity, his honesty, and his courage, was a hero not a saint—that is, the character was explicable on humanistic presuppositions. Sir J. M. Barrie's *The Little Minister* might be taken as an example of a novel where a saccharine sentimentality makes the clerical character quite incredible.

If hagiography is to be avoided, so equally is secular caricature. That is why the leading clerical characters of Sinclair Lewis and W. Somerset Maugham are unacceptable. They are too obviously stock figures, so utterly at variance with the standards and beliefs of their profession, and so completely earthy that it is difficult to believe that they ever thought they were entrusted with the Gospel. If hagiography errs because it is never human enough, caricature in religious fiction errs because its depravity is unalloyed with the divine dissatisfaction. The very snobbishness of Maugham's medical missionaries, the Davidsons, is out of keeping with their combined professions: the ministry and medicine. The same writer's vicar, the Rev. William Carey, seems the more incredible because he is shown as being a tongue-tied man with a very limited vocabulary and a great buyer of second-hand books which he never reads. The far likelier defect of a minister is an incontinence of speech, an irrepressible gift of gab. Moreover, while it is poverty that forces so many ministers to buy second-hand books, I have never heard of one who did not read them with the utmost voracity. The greatest caricature of all is, of course, Elmer Gantry. He is a compound of the seven deadly sins (sloth excepted), and what is hardest to accept is the implication that he was never visited by qualms of conscience. If the whiteness of hagiography is unlikely, the unrelieved blackness of the caricature of men who had sought to live the altruistic life is even more improbable.

This leads to the conviction that a good religious novel must be a portrait in chiaroscuro—a study of blacks and whites, with the white gradually prevailing by the grace of God. It is this which makes the character of Hester in *The Scarlet Letter* so impressive as she makes a constructive application of tragedy in which her own frailty and her need of the divine forgiveness blossom into charity for others. It is the painfully won victories of grace over sin in the Catholic novelists that make the country priest of Bernanos, the abbé Calou of Mauriac, and the whisky priest of Graham Greene so real and so significant. It is the same unobtrusive but deep belief in the providence of God that makes Cudlipp's ministry in *Men and Brethren* a drudgery that is also divine. By giving the human scene the eschatological backcloth of Heaven and Hell, the religious writer sees that apparently trivial actions of men and women have abiding consequences unperceived by the humanist. This makes Alan Paton's story of a Zulu pastor in search of a lost son also the parable of the Divine Father in search of the lost soul. Unless a novel includes these dimensions of sin and grace, time and eternity, it cannot be considered a religious novel of any significance.

The theology need not, indeed, *should* not obtrude; but the account of human nature and destiny must be, in the last analysis, theological. That is, its estimate of man must be that of Christian realism: it will be prevented from shallow optimism and sentimentalism by the recollection of the Cross; it will also be guarded against a despairing pessimism by the remembrance of the Resurrection. Man, therefore, is acknowledged as a crucifier who is redeemable. Moreover, the Christian novelist knows that while heredity, environment, and education, all play their significant parts in the destiny of men, the ultimate power is the grace of God. Like the dying country priest of Bernanos, he confesses that 'Grace is everywhere.' In fulfilling these canons of criticism, quite apart from their innate artistry, I believe that *The Scarlet Letter, The Diary of a Country Priest, The Woman of the Pharisees, The Power and the Glory, Men and Brethren,* and *Cry, the Beloved Country* are distinguished *religious* novels. They each show the role of Divine Providence and Grace. This Augustinian interpretation is strongly in the foreground of *The Power and the Glory* where the whisky priest is God's marked man, whereas it is revealed only at the conclusion of Cozzens' novel, *Men and Brethren.* The category of Divine election is basic in Bernanos, Mauriac, and Paton, and curiously it is present (even if considered an illusion by

Maugham) in the Dr. Davidson of the short story *Rain*. Moreover, each of the novels mentioned depicts the pride which
ultimately yields to humility only by the victory of sovereign
grace. Street's novels, as also *One Foot in Heaven*, show realisti-
cally the irritations and difficulties of the religious life, but not
the abysses of despair nor the ascents of grace. The three novelists who deal with the problem of the loss of faith are indeed
concerned with a profoundly religious theme, but they did not
produce distinguished religious novels because, in the case of
Robert Elsmere and of the 'Mark Rutherford' novels, the ultimate answer is anthropocentric not theocentric, and, in the
case of the third, *The Damnation of Theron Ware*, the problem
is bypassed by the assumption that doubt is necessarily dishonest.

II

It will at once be apparent that Catholic priests seem to have
been more successfully delineated than Protestant ministers.
The successful portraits of the country priest, the abbé Calou,
and the whisky priest can be matched only by Cozzens' Ernest
Cudlipp and Paton's Father Vincent and Stephen Kumalo, and
yet only four of the fifteen novelists considered were Roman
Catholics. However, the disparity is not so great if it is remembered that of the remaining eleven novelists four were
probably agnostics.

In partial explanation of the discrepancy two important factors must be borne in mind. The first is that the portrayal of the
Catholic priest in fiction has much greater apparent dramatic
possibilities than that of his Protestant counterpart. He is, in
the first place, immediately identifiable by his distinctive dress
in a way that Protestant ministers (with the exception of Episcopalians) are not. The higher he is in the Catholic hierarchy

the more distinctive is his every day habit and the more splendid
are his liturgical garments. His functions as the celebrant of the
Mass and as the director of souls in the confessional box are, in
their respective publicity and privacy, much more exciting in
their potentialities for description than the Protestant parson
preaching in the pulpit or counseling in the study. The Roman
Catholic priest has a magisterial authority of a superior order,
the Protestant parson has only a ministerial authority. Furthermore, the Catholic priest, monk, friar, or nun, is mysteriously
set apart from the rest of humanity by the vow of celibacy—
itself the claim to a higher vocation. The Protestant doctrine of
the priesthood of all believers means that the Protestant minister
can never be more than a *primus inter pares*; one who is involved
in marriage and in the joys and anxieties of married life cannot
appear to be a superior type of humanity. Nor is this his wish.
In the same way, the celibacy of the priest gives him a mobility
and an availability that is superior to that of the Protestant
minister. In all these ways the priest is potentially a more
exciting character than the Protestant clergyman.

Protestant clergy, in the contemporary scene at least, are
less congenial subjects for literary portraiture for another reason: Protestantism is so often represented in terms not of a
religion based on revelation (with the correlates of sin and
salvation) but as a moralism of respectability. The bourgeois
and middle-class complexion of so much Protestantism seems to
imply that the function of the ministry is the raising of morale
and the sanctification of the *status quo,* and that this requires a
cadre of safe, dull, timid 'yes-men.' By contrast, Catholicism is
never likely to appear as the sanctification of the English or
American way of life. Its multi-racial and international composition, its Italian connections, and its crossing of class and
color lines give it an exotic character, while its unrelenting, if
naïvely truculent, verbal warfare with Communism as godless-

ness makes it appear as a crusade in the twentieth century. Its definite dogmas and objective channels of grace contrast so effectively with the often hesitant and usually undemonstrative nature of Protestant faith. Moreover, Catholicism is so explicit and Protestantism (with its private judgment) so implicit. One has only to compare Protestantism's insistence that right motives in ethical action are known only to God and the individual with Catholicism's ecclesiastical penances, or the publicity of the Catholic prelate with the relative privacy of the Protestant minister who would be indistinguishable from any layman in the street, for the point to be appreciated. In short, in terms of artistic difficulty a Protestant parson is much harder to portray than a Catholic priest.

Nonetheless one single theme may be said to characterise the successful Catholic and Protestant portraits of clergymen which we have glimpsed in these pages: the true servant of Christ and the Church counts the world well lost. God's minister must be, like Athanasius, *contra mundum*. This is the true, the authentic apostolical succession. Bernanos' country priest recognizes that prudence and faith must be enemies; Mauriac's Calou loses his seminary chair and even his insignificant cure of souls in the wilderness because he has been reported to his archbishop by a female Pharisee, yet feels this is no more than his desert; Greene's whisky priest, like the Master he increasingly serves with fidelity, is 'despised and rejected of man'; Cozzens' Cudlipp knows that charity and truth have so overcome tact and expediency in him that he will never attain success as the world understands the term and that there are no ecclesiastical plums in store for him; Paton's Stephen Kumalo is a faithful but very bewildered man of God, naïve to the cynic but deeply devout, like Johnston, Cozzens' returned Alaskan missionary. In all Christian communions the saint must appear unorthodox in his charity, because he is truly following his Lord who was accused of frequenting the company of publicans and sinners. Whether the risk he runs be death as in *The Power and the Glory*, or the ridicule of the conventional and the respectable as in *The Diary of a Country Priest*, *The Woman of the Pharisees*, and, to a lesser degree, in *The Gauntlet* and in *One Foot in Heaven*, the price of fidelity to Christ is nonconformity with the world.

The complementary truth is that the most tragic failures in the ministry and the priesthood are those who succumb to the blandishments of the world. The greater the caricature of the ministry the cruder is the temptation and the quicker the fall. Maugham in *Rain*, Sinclair Lewis in *Elmer Gantry*, and Cronin in *Grand Canary* automatically assume that *eros* will vanquish *agape* whenever they meet. More subtly, Hawthorne suggests in *The Scarlet Letter* that there is an affinity between divine and human love and that a rigorous, legalistic, and unforgiving society is preparing whips with which to lash its own back; but all the same Dimmesdale's fatal flaw is adultery and yet the adulteress triumphs over the society that condemns her because of her own forgiving and charitable nature. Repentance and the growth of a deep charity are not serious possibilities in the thought of the caricaturists of religion.

Hardly less crude is the fatal defect of conceit as pictured in Maugham's *Of Human Bondage*, in which the opinionated Rev. William Carey is conscious only of his social position and the deference due to him (his only concern at his wife's funeral is to see that the number of floral memorials is greater than that at the funeral of a neighboring vicar's wife), and who seems to believe that he has a divine right to treat his wife and ward as menials. More serious, however, is his tendency to give a trivial answer to a serious question. But all the time one asks: How could so conceited a man ever have entered far less remained in the ministry? Intellectual pride, dissolving moral absolutes into relativities, is the fatal flaw in Theron Ware. De Vries' Mackerel is more credible as an aesthetic and intellectual snob, but possibly less heinous than Mr. Carey, because presumably the People's Liberal Church of which he is minister is a community that consciously attempts to liberate itself from the shackles of Christian orthodoxy.

The far subtler temptations to conceit are more nebulous than a conflict between the doctrinal standards of the Church and the belief of the minister. This is, indeed, a real and urgent problem, as Street shows in *The Gauntlet* and Harold Frederic shows in *The Damnation of Theron Ware*. The really testing conflicts are, however, the subtler antagonisms between truth and tact, between Christian charity and expediency, and between the pressures of fidelity to God and fulfilling popular expectation. It is in the exploration of these dilemmas that the subtlety of the best religious novelists is to be discovered. The country priest has to learn the hard lesson that he cannot hope for popularity, for this would be to make his charges love him not his Master. The measure of the shoddiness of Elmer Gantry's ministerial life is that his sensationalism provides what his congregations want, not what they need. Cudlipp's greatness is seen in his persistent care and concern for the Bohemians, the decadent, and the shiftless, as in his willingness to stand by a promise to permit a rabbi to preach in his pulpit, despite the opposition of his bishop and the advice of his all-too-expedient rector. Mark Rutherford and Robert Elsmere win our admiration by the way they leave the securities to follow the truth. It is fatally easy, our novelists would suggest, to compromise the truth by ambiguity. The fault of Robert Tranter, Theron Ware, and Mackerel, as well as Anselm Mealey is that they exploit their people, as they exploit their own personalities. In Tranter's infamous words: 'Personality counts in business everywhere. . . . I'll say it counts double in the biggest business deal in life. And that, Sue, is putting over the Word of God.' The most dangerous as well as the most common temptation in the ministry is that of popularity with all its ramifications. It includes the perils of preaching that is not meant to offend (which, having no judgment, has no mercy), of a quantitative and statistical assessal of the work of God, of judging people by appearances, of degenerating from a minister of the Word of God into a mere master of ceremonies, and of the terrible distortion that commends faith in God because of its by-products, such as emotional security, mental health, morale, the confidence that brings business success, and getting in with the right set of people. The ultimate blasphemy is to make a convenience of God or His people.

Our novelists describe not only the temptations, but also the difficulties of the ministry. Street in particular exposes the goldfish-bowl life a minister leads, in which not only his own actions but those of his wife and children are under constant scrutiny and subject to the frequent misunderstanding by the malevolent. Hartzell Spence never allows us to forget the pathetic shifts by which his parents had to overcome the penury of the Methodist parsonage. Cozzens gives us a poignant glimpse of Johnston the missionary returned from Alaska with only a few photographs, a Bible, and a copy of the *Imitation of Christ*, in his barely furnished room and makes the perfect comment: 'The rewards of his hard, bare, devoted life, the unsearchable riches of Christ, were given him in the perfect freedom and perfect joy of needing nothing.' The same author shows us that his vicar has an exhausting life, punctuated by the ringing of the insistent telephone bell, calling him on duty at all hours of the day or night, and without a fee, which is, by contrast, the medical doctor's reward. Spence and Street illustrate abundantly the multifarious duties of the minister, the irritating vexations and disappointments, the burdensome daily round of duty with its commonplace calls, committees, and church suppers, and the sordidness of sickness and approaching death, which claim so much of his time. Street's novels are an astonishing record of the days of small things that engross a minister's life, which only a sympathetic identification with the needs of others can make endurable.

The novelists have treated the temptations and the difficulties of the ministry. Have they also chronicled its achievements? Apart from the caricaturists, for whom the ministry is a parasitical vocation (the retelling of myths) partly redeemed by the inculcation of morality or the practice of benevolence, the answer is, Yes. The glory of the ministry or the priesthood is to be found in its calling to men to search for the image of the King in the debased currency of humanity—in the country priest's fight for the soul of the countess, in Calou's conviction that the female Pharisee is no blinder to the ways of God than he is and equally worthy of redemption, in Cudlipp's love for the unloved (irrespective of any natural affection), and in Father Vincent's patient restoration of the distracted Kumalo's faith. The minister and the priest are for the religious novelists God's elect, God's marked men, the channels for the amazing mercy of God Himself. They reduce the sneers of the cynic and the selfishness of the sentimentalist to absurd irrelevance with their combination of unshockableness (for they know the pitiable attempts sin makes to appear beguiling) and faith (for they are aware that miracles of grace have been accomplished in themselves). They confront the Titanism of the proud (and their assumption of a superior knowledge of the ways of the world) with the terrible, unbreakable meekness of the humble. They meet pride with simplicity, devious illusions with direct truth. While the deserving fickle come complaining to them of the hardships of life and parading their luxuries of doubt and disbelief, themselves they bear all the slings and arrows of outrageous fortune as privileges, as the scars of the veterans entering into the fellowship of Christ's sufferings. This the country priest, the abbé

Calou, and Father Vincent know; but the whisky priest is too humble to think of himself except in the company of Judas. From their faith is born not only humility and grateful endurance but also courage and charity. The ignorant country priest, though quaking, receives all the taunts of the enraged and humiliated countess, because he merely fulfills his God-commanded charge. The whisky priest, apologizing to the firing squad for the inconvenience he is causing them, sought this terrible death convinced that God willed it. And all of them, true minister and true priest alike, become not so much mirrors of the grace of God, but windows through which, like the largesse of golden light, His spendthrift and uncalculating charity is thrown to the undeserving. They know, to change the metaphor, that they are the beagles of the invisible hunter, God, who is lightning and love, judgment and mercy. The greatest religious novelists know that this is the supreme privilege and glory of the Christian ministry and priesthood.

The measure of the finest portraits of the ministry is that they show the reality of the temptations which assail the servants of God and the greatness of the grace which overcomes them. If the earthiness of the vessel is all they see, they are only caricaturists. If the treasure of the Gospel alone is shown in their portraits, apart from the clay vessel, they are hagiographers and sentimentalists. But if they portray the ministry and priesthood in its squalor and grandeur, its earthiness and its treasure, they have succeeded in a most difficult and worthwhile enterprise. For the delineation of the squalor is a warning, and the portrayal of the grandeur is an encouragement which only the Christian artist can provide.

BIBLIOGRAPHY

Bibliography

I. *A Chronology of the Novels Discussed:*

1850 Nathaniel Hawthorne *The Scarlet Letter*

1881 William Hale White *The Autobiography of Mark Ruther-ford*

1885 William Hale White *Mark Rutherford's Deliverance*

1888 Mrs. Humphry Ward *Robert Elsmere*

1896 Harold Frederic *The Damnation of Theron Ware, or Illumination*

1915 W. Somerset Maugham *Of Human Bondage*

1919 W. Somerset Maugham *Rain*

1927 Sinclair Lewis *Elmer Gantry*

1933 Anthony Joseph Cronin *Grand Canary*

1936 Georges Bernanos *Le Journal d'un curé de campagne* (English trans. 1937: *The Diary of a Country Priest*)

1936 James Gould Cozzens *Men and Brethren*

1940 Graham Greene *The Power and the* Glory (original American title: *The Labyrinthine Ways*)

1940 Hartzell Spence *One Foot in Heaven*

1941 Anthony Joseph Cronin *The Keys of the Kingdom*

1941 François Mauriac *La Pharisienne* (English trans. 1946: *A Woman of the Pharisees*)

1945 James Howell Street *The Gauntlet*

1948 Alan Paton *Cry, the Beloved Country*

1949   Sinclair Lewis   *The God-Seeker*

1951   James Howell Street   *The High Calling*

1958   Peter De Vries   *The Mackerel Plaza*

II. *A Select Bibliography of the Novelists and Their Interpreters.*

(The names of the novelists appear in capitals, their interpreters in lower case.)

Allott, Kenneth and Farris, Miriam   *The Art of Graham Greene* (Hamilton, London: 1951)

Balthasar, Hans Urs von   *Bernanos* (Hegner, Koln: 1956; trans. as *Le Chrétien Bernanos*, du Seuil, Paris: 1956)

B E R N A N O S, G E O R G E S: *Journal d'un curé de campagne* (Plon, Paris: 1936) *The Diary of a Country Priest* trans. from the French by Pamela Morris, Macmillan, New York: 1937)

Brophy, John   *Somerset Maugham* (publ. for the British Council by Longmans, London, etc.: 1952)

Chrétien, Louis Émile   *La Pensée morale de Nathaniel Hawthorne . . .* (Didier, Paris: 1932)

Cormeau, Nelly   *L'art de François Mauriac* (Grasset, Paris: 1951)

C O Z Z E N S, J A M E S   G O U L D: *By Love Possessed* (Harcourt, Brace, New York: 1957) *Men and Brethren* (Harcourt, Brace, New York: 1936)

Critique   James Gould Cozzens, Minneapolis, Vol. 1, No. 3, Winter, 1958

C R O N I N, A N T H O N Y   J O S E P H: *Adventures between Two Worlds* (McGraw-Hill, New York: 1952)
Grand Canary (Little, Brown, Boston: 1933)
The Keys of the Kingdom (Little, Brown, Boston: 1941)

Curch, William *The Emergence, Rise and Decline of the Reputation of Sinclair Lewis.* (Microfilm, Chicago University doctoral dissertations, 1954, Reel 18.)

Davies, Horton '*Alan Paton: Literary Artist and Anglican*', art. in *The Hibbert Journal*, London and Boston, Vol. L, April, 1952, pp. 262–8.

DE VRIES, PETER: *The Mackerel Plaza* (Little, Brown, Boston: 1958)

Fick, Leonard J. *The Light Beyond: a Study of Hawthorne's Theology* (Newman Press, Westminster, Md.: 1955)

FREDERIC, HAROLD: *The Damnation of Theron Ware, or Illumination* (Kimball and Stone, New York: 1896)

Gladstone, William Ewart '*Robert Elsmere' and the Battle of Belief*, art. in *The Nineteenth Century*, London, May, 1888.

GREENE, GRAHAM: *Brighton Rock* (Viking, New York: 1938)
The Lawless Roads (Eyre, London: 1939)
The Lost Childhood (Eyre, London: 1951)
The Power and the Glory (first publ. in the U.S.A. as *The Labyrinthine Ways*, Viking, New York: 1940)

HAWTHORNE, NATHANIEL: *The Scarlet Letter* (1st. ed. Ticknor, Boston: 1850; ed. consulted, The Modern Library, New York: 1945)

Hourdin, Georges *Mauriac, romancier chrétien* (du temps présent, Paris: 1945)

Jarrett-Kerr, Martin *François Mauriac* (Bowes, Cambridge: 1954)

Jonas, Klaus *The Gentleman from Cap Ferrat* (New Haven, Conn., Center of Maugham Studies: 1956)

LEWIS, SINCLAIR: *Elmer Gantry* (Harcourt, Brace, New York: 1927) *The God-seeker* (Random House, New York: 1949)

Madaule, Jacques *Graham Greene* ... (du temps présent, Paris: 1949)

MAUGHAM, W. SOMERSET: *The Complete Short Stories of W.*

    Somerset Maugham (2 vols., of which 1. includes *Rain*, Doubleday, New York: 1952)
    Of Human Bondage (The Modern Library, New York: 1915)

M A U R I A C , F R A N Ç O I S : *La Pharisienne* (Grasset, Paris: 1941)
    A Woman of the Pharisees (trans. from the French by Gerard Hopkins, Eyre, London: 1946)
    Mes Grands Hommes (du Rocher, Monaco: 1949; trans. from French by Elsie Pell as *Men I Hold Great*. Philosophical Library, New York: 1951)

Miller, Alexander   *The Renewal of Man; A Twentieth-Century Essay on Justification by Faith* (Doubleday, New York: 1955)

O'Donnell, Donat   *Maria Cross; Imaginative Patterns in a Group of Modern Catholic Writers* (Oxford University Press, New York: 1952)

Parrish, James A.   *James Gould Cozzens: A Critical Analysis.* (University Microfilms, Ann Arbor, Michigan. Doctoral dissertation series No: 14, 169. Original Ph.D. thesis in Florida State University Library)

P A T O N , A L A N : *Cry, the Beloved Country* (Cape, London: 1948, Scribners, New York: 1948)
    Too Late the Phalarope (Cape, London: 1951, Scribners, New York: 1951)

Rischik, Josef   *Graham Greene und sein Werk* (Francke, Bern: 1951)

S P E N C E , H A R T Z E L L : *Get Thee Behind Me; My Life as a Preacher's Son* (McGraw-Hill, New York: 1942)
    One Foot in Heaven (McGraw-Hill, New York: 1940)

S T E V E N S O N , R O B E R T L O U I S : *Vailima Letters* (2 vols., Chicago: 1895)

Stock, Irvine   *William Hale White (Mark Rutherford), A Critical Study* (Columbia University Press, New York: 1956)

Stone, Wilfred   *Religion and Art of William Hale White ('Mark Rutherford')* (Stanford University Press, California: 1954)

STREET, JAMES HOWELL: *The Gauntlet* (Doubleday, New York: 1945)
The High Calling (Doubleday, New York: 1951)

Taylor, A. E. 'The Novels of Mark Rutherford,' art. in *Essays and Studies*, Vol. 5, 1914, published by Oxford University Press, London, pp. 51–74.

Trevelyan, Janet Penrose *The Life of Mrs. Humphry Ward by Her Daughter* . . . (Constable, London: 1923)

Van Doren, Carl Clinton *Sinclair Lewis, A Biographical Sketch* (Doubleday, New York: 1933)

Walters, J. Stuart *Mrs. Humphry Ward and the Trend of Ethical Development since Robert Elsmere* (Paul, London: 1912)

WARD, MARY AUGUSTA (ARNOLD): *A Writer's Recollections* (Collins, London: 1918) 'Mrs. Humphry Ward'
Robert Elsmere (2 vols., Macmillan, London and New York: 1888)

White, Mrs. Dorothy V. *Last Pages of a Journal, with Other Papers by Mark Rutherford* (Oxford University Press, London: 1915)

WHITE, WILLIAM HALE: *The Autobiography of Mark Rutherford* (T. Fisher Unwin, London: 1881)
Mark Rutherford's Deliverance (T. Fisher Unwin, London: 1885)

Wyndham, Francis *Graham Greene* (publ. for the British Council by Longmans, London: 1955)

NOTES

Notes

CHAPTER I

1. *Poetical Fragments* (Parkhurst, London, 1699), p. 30.

CHAPTER II

1. *The Scarlet Letter* (Modern Library edition, Random House, New York, 1937), p. 225.

2. Ibid. p. 167 f.

3. Ibid.

4. Ibid. p. 156.

5. *Elmer Gantry* (Harcourt, Brace and Co., New York, 1927), p. 1.

6. Ibid. p. 26.

7. Ibid. p. 30.

8. Ibid. p. 32.

9. Ibid. p. 38.

10. Ibid. p. 73.

11. Ibid. p. 342.

12. Ibid. p. 358.

13. *The God-Seeker* (Random House, New York, 1949), pp. 11-13.

14. Ibid. pp. 137-8.

15. Ibid. p. 266.

16. Both were published by Doubleday and Company, Inc., New York.

17. *The Gauntlet*, p. 19.

18. Ibid. pp. 174-5.

19. Ibid. p. 250.

20. *The High Calling*, pp. 46 f.

21. Ibid. p. 252.

22. Ibid. pp. 256-7.

CHAPTER III

1. The first novel and its sequel were published by T. Fisher Unwin of London, and all references are to the first editions.

2. *The Autobiography of Mark Rutherford*, p. 7.

3. Ibid. p. 7.

4. Ibid. p. 22.

5. Ibid. p. 35.

6. Ibid. p. 54.

7. Ibid. p. 78.

8. Ibid. p. 82.

9. Ibid. pp. 87-8.

10. Ibid. p. 100.

11. Ibid. p. 111.

12. *Mark Rutherford's Deliverance*, p. 109.

13. *The Autobiography of Mark Rutherford*, p. 132.

14. Ibid. p. 133.

15. *Mark Rutherford's Deliverance*, p. 12.

16. Ibid. pp. 27-9.

17. Ibid. p. 65. Cf. also p. 25 for a more horrific account of squalor.

18. *The Autobiography of Mark Rutherford*, p. 10.

19. *Mark Rutherford's Deliverance*, pp. 90-91.

20. Ibid.

21. *Robert Elsmere* (2 vols., Macmillan, London & New York, 1888), I, p. 95.

22. Ibid. I, p. 124.

23. Ibid. I, p. 99.

24. Ibid. I, p. 248.

25. Ibid. II, pp. 36-7.

26. Ibid. II, pp. 18-19.

27. Ibid. II, p. 24.

28. Ibid. I, p. 196.

29. Ibid. II, p. 56f.

30. Ibid. II, pp. 74-5. One may note the correspondence of the final affirmation with Tennyson's lines: (Prologue to *In Memoriam*.)

> 'Our little systems have their day;
> They have their day and cease to be:
> They are but broken light of thee,
> And thou, O Lord, art more than they.'

31. Ibid. II, p. 372.

32. Ibid. II, p. 411.

33. Published by Stone and Kimball, New York, 1896. All references are to this, the first edition.

34. *The Damnation of Theron Ware, or Illumination*, pp. 7-8.

35. Ibid. pp. 42-3.

36. Ibid. pp. 42-3.

37. Ibid. p. 107.

38. Ibid. pp. 198-9.

39. Ibid. p. 346.

40. Ibid. p. 359.

41. Ibid. pp. 478-9.

CHAPTER IV

1. See Alexander Miller, *The Renewal of Man* (Doubleday, New York, 1955), pp. 28-34.

2. *The Diary of a Country Priest* (tr. by Pamela Morris, Macmillan, New York, 1937), p. 3.

3. The French original reads: 'Calculer nos chances, a quoi bon? On ne joue pas contre Dieu.' English translation, pp. 5-6.

4. Op. cit. p. 18.

5. Ibid. pp. 11-13.

6. Ibid. pp. 27-8.

7. The explosive French original reads thus: 'Un prêtre qui descende de la chaire de Vérité, la bouche en machin de poule, un peu échauffé, mais content, il n'a pas prêché, il a ronronné, tout au plus.'

8. Op. cit. p. 54.

9. Ibid. p. 91.

10. Ibid. p. 199.

11. Ibid. pp. 279-80.

12. Ibid. p. 298.

13. Ibid. p. 174.

14. The present writer's translation from the original French, published by Editions du Seuil, Paris, 1954, p. 152.

15. Trans. Gerard Hopkins, published by Eyre and Spottiswoode, London, 1946.

16. *L'Art de François Mauriac*, (Grasset, Paris, 1951), p. 164. The citation is translated by the present writer.

17. In the original French the definition reads: 'il marche devant la Grace comme le chien précède le chasseur invisible.'

18. Op. cit. p. 47.

19. Ibid. p. 107.

20. Ibid. p. 108.

21. Ibid. p. 144.

22. Ibid. p. 152.

23. Ibid. p. 176.

24. Ibid. p. 177.

25. Ibid. pp. 177-8.

26. Ibid. p. 185.

27. Ibid. p. 203.

28. References are to the fifth printing, published by the Viking Press, New York, 1951.

29. Op. cit. p. 128.

30. *The Lawless Roads,* pp. 50-51.

31. Op. cit. pp. 44-5.

32. Ibid. p. 32.

33. *Mes Grands Hommes* tr. Elsie Pell, as *Men I Hold Great* (Philosophical Library, New York, 1951), pp. 124 f.

34. Ibid.

35. *The Power and the Glory,* p. 29.

36. Ibid. p. 32.

37. Ibid. pp. 53-4.

38. Ibid. p. 111.

39. Ibid. p. 177.

40. Ibid. pp. 232-3.

41. Ibid. p. 239.

42. Ibid. p. 280.

43. Ibid. p. 294.

44. Ibid. p. 298.

45. Ibid p. 301.

CHAPTER V

1. Its subtitle is 'Being Correspondence addressed by Robert Louis Stevenson to Sidney Colvin, November 1890–October 1894,' (2 vols., Chicago 1895). The references are to Vol. I, pp 81-2 and I, 57, respectively. I owe these references to the kindness of the missionary statesman and historian, the Rev. Dr. Norman Goodall of Benson, near Oxford.

2. See Richard Wright's *Native Son* and Lillian Smith's *Strange Fruit.*

3. P. 2. All references to *Rain* are to *The Complete Short Stories of W. Somerset Maugham* (Vol. I, East and West, Doubleday and Company, Inc., New York, 1952.)

4. Ibid. p. 11.

5. Ibid. p. 39.

6. See John Brophy's *Somerset Maugham* (British Council, London, New York and Toronto, 1952), p. 15.

7. *Of Human Bondage*, p. 13. (References are to The Modern Library Edition, Random House, New York.)

8. Ibid. p. 14.

9. Ibid. p. 310.

10. Ibid. p. 541.

11. His religious pilgrimage and philosophy are found in *Adventures in Two Worlds* (McGraw-Hill, New York, 1952).

12. *Grand Canary*, p. 27. References are to the edition published by Little, Brown and Company, Boston, 1933.

13. Ibid. p. 245.

14. *The Keys of the Kingdom*, p. 331, published by Little, Brown and Company, Boston, 1941.

15. Ibid. p. 343.

16. Ibid. p. 144.

17. Ibid. p. 212.

18. *Cry, the Beloved Country* (Scribner's, New York; Jonathan Cape, London, 1948), p. 20.

19. Ibid. p. 28.

20. Ibid. p. 30.

21. Ibid. p. 42.

22. Ibid. p. 145.

23. Ibid. p. 102.

24. Ibid. pp. 102-3.

25. Ibid. p. 104.

26. Ibid.

27. For Paton's theological background see the present writer's article, *Alan Paton: Literary Artist and Anglican,* in *The Hibbert Journal,* vol. L, No. 198, April 1952, London and Boston, pp. 262-8.

CHAPTER VI

1. See the centennial edition of *The Autobiography of Peter Cartwright,* published by Abingdon-Cokesbury, New York and Nashville.

2. *The Kingdom of God in America* (1935, re-issued 1956, Shoe String Press, Hamden, Conn.), p. 193.

3. *One Foot in Heaven, the Life of a Practical Parson* (McGraw-Hill, New York), p. 4.

4. Ibid. p. 9.

5. Ibid.

6. For a Congregational confirmation of the necessity to adopt such ruses to eke out a minister's resources, see Roland H. Bainton's delightful study of his father, *Pilgrim Parson* (Nelson, New York and Edinburgh, 1958), p. 99.

7. *One Foot in Heaven,* p. 131.

8. Ibid. p. 5.

9. Ibid. p. 191.

10. Ibid. p. 116.

11. Ibid. p. 118.

12. Ibid. p. 122.

13. Ibid. p. 132.

14. Ibid. p. 183.

15. Ibid. p. 185.

16. *Men and Brethren,* (Harcourt, Brace and Company, New York, 1936) p. 272.

17. Ibid. p. 195.

18. Ibid. pp. 197-8.

19. See Dwight McDonald's swashbuckling article *By Cozzens Possessed* in the January 1958 issue of *Commentary;* also *Critique: Studies in Modern Fiction,* Vol. I, No. 3, Winter 1958, Minneapolis.

20. *Men and Brethren*, pp. 26-7.

21. Ibid. p. 47.

22. Ibid. pp. 16-17.

23. Ibid. pp. 280-81.

24. *By Love Possessed* (Harcourt, Brace and Company, New York, 1957), p. 351.

25. *The Mackerel Plaza* (Little, Brown and Company, Boston, 1958), p. 4.

26. Ibid. p. 5.

27. Ibid. pp. 10-11.

28. Ibid. pp. 27-9.

29. Ibid. pp. 7-8.

30. Ibid. p. 188.

31. Ibid. p. 30f.

32. Ibid. p. 258.

INDEX

Index